T0334640

# Cambridge Elements ≡

Elements in Sign Languages
edited by
Erin Wilkinson
*University of New Mexico*
David Quinto-Pozos
*University of Texas at Austin*

# CREATIVE SIGN LANGUAGE

Rachel Sutton-Spence
*Federal University of Santa Catarina*
Fernanda de Araújo Machado
*Federal University of Santa Catarina*

## CAMBRIDGE
### UNIVERSITY PRESS

Shaftesbury Road, Cambridge CB2 8EA, United Kingdom

One Liberty Plaza, 20th Floor, New York, NY 10006, USA

477 Williamstown Road, Port Melbourne, VIC 3207, Australia

314–321, 3rd Floor, Plot 3, Splendor Forum, Jasola District Centre, New Delhi – 110025, India

103 Penang Road, #05–06/07, Visioncrest Commercial, Singapore 238467

Cambridge University Press is part of Cambridge University Press & Assessment, a department of the University of Cambridge.

We share the University's mission to contribute to society through the pursuit of education, learning and research at the highest international levels of excellence.

www.cambridge.org
Information on this title: www.cambridge.org/9781009344876

DOI: 10.1017/9781009344883

First published 2023

*A catalogue record for this publication is available from the British Library*

ISBN 978-1-009-34487-6 Paperback
ISSN 2752-9401 (online)
ISSN 2752-9398 (print)

# Creative Sign Language

Elements in Sign Languages

DOI: 10.1017/9781009344883
First published online: August 2023

Rachel Sutton-Spence
*Federal University of Santa Catarina*

Fernanda de Araújo Machado
*Federal University of Santa Catarina*

**Author for correspondence:** Rachel Sutton-Spence, suttonspence@gmail.com

**Abstract:** This Element describes creative sign language in deaf literature. To showcase the exciting developments in Latin American deaf literature, the authors focus upon creative Libras as it is used by the Brazilian deaf community while emphasising aspects of Libras literature that can be seen in similar productions and performances in sign language literatures around the world. Throughout the Element, the authors refer to examples of Libras poems and stories to give readers a practical experience of appreciating works of creative sign language. They describe Libras literature within its historical and social contexts and consider questions of performance, filming and editing, and the potential for written Libras literature. Drawing on anthologies of Libras poems, jokes, and stories, they use close-reading techniques to show how the literary effects are created while reminding the reader that sign language literature cannot be separated from the deaf community.

This Element also has a video abstract: www.cambridge.org/creativesignlanguage

**Keywords:** sign language literature, deaf literature, creative sign language, sign language performance, deaf culture

ISBNs: 9781009344876 (PB), 9781009344883 (OC)
ISSNs: 2752-9401 (online), 2752-9398 (print)

# Contents

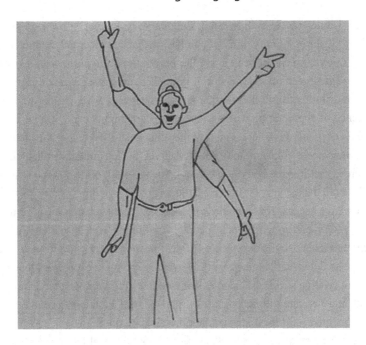

*Four Arms Language.*[1]

> *I can play with language!*
> *Language! Language!*
> *Language! Language! Language! Language! Language! Language!*

'Poetry' by the Flying Words Project, Peter Cook and Kenny Lerner (1993 – reproduced in Nathan Lerner and Feigel 2009, in American Sign Language (ASL) and English)

## Introduction

> *Hold a tree in the palm of your hand,*
> *or topple it with a crash.*
> *Sail a boat on finger waves,*
> *or sink it with a splash.*
> *From your fingertips see a frog leap,*
> *at a passing butterfly.*
> *The word becomes the picture in this language for the eye.*
> 'Language for the Eye' by Dorothy Miles (1976)

This Element describes creative sign language in deaf literature. To showcase the exciting developments in Latin American deaf literature, we focus upon

---

[1] Painting by Fernanda Machado, after 'Poetry' by the Flying Words Project, Peter Cook and Kenny Lerner (1993).

creative Libras (as Brazilian Sign Language is known) produced by the Brazilian deaf community, but we emphasise that the essential characteristics of Libras literature can be seen in similar productions and performances in sign language literatures around the world. In this Element, we include examples of poems and stories from several other sign languages to give readers a practical experience of appreciating works of creative sign language.[2]

The focus of our work here is on deaf literature in sign language. Any definition of literature needs to accommodate exceptions, but our understanding of deaf literature is that it is the body of creative language work of deaf communities. It includes both fiction and non-fiction, in the form of storytelling, poetry, jokes, and other creative pieces. It is founded on four key characteristics: it is primarily created and/or performed by deaf people, it is aimed at deaf audiences, it has content that relates to the experiences of deaf people, and it is performed in sign language as the visual language of deaf people. There are exceptions to each of these four criteria, so we see examples of creative sign language that do not fulfil all four and yet can still be considered part of deaf literature, but the general parameters are useful for understanding this field of study.

We describe creative sign language within its historical and social contexts, tracing its development within the national deaf community and mainstream society, as well as the influence of deaf artists and performers from other countries. The role of linguistic, social, and education policies in promoting creative sign language will be outlined, as they impact on the development of sign language artists, artworks, and audiences. We also trace the effect that changes in technology and the transmission of creative sign language via the internet and social media have had on the artform, considering questions of performance, filming and editing, and the potential for written sign language literature.

Following an in-depth exploration of the ways that aesthetic sign language is used to create highly valued, visually intense, emotionally rich poems and stories, we will consider emerging genres of deaf literature. Questions of original deaf literature for children and the role of translated, retold, or adapted stories from books and films will be addressed. Drawing on anthologies of Libras poems, jokes, and stories, we will use close-reading techniques to show how the literary effects are created, while reminding the reader that creative sign language in any country cannot be separated from the deaf community. The

---

[2] It is impossible in this single Element to do justice to the rich production of creative sign language by deaf artists around the world. We focus here on Libras but also refer to work by artists from the USA, Italy, Germany, and the United Kingdom, because we have studied them, having access to their material, but there are many more examples from countries that are not included here. All we can do is encourage readers to look for sign language artists working in their own deaf communities. The work will be there and will repay study.

themes addressed in different genres provide strong insights into the complex identities of deaf people in the twenty-first century, always celebrating the beauty, richness, and sheer delight of this form of deaf cultural heritage.

# 1 History and Social Context of Sign Language Literature

There are deaf artists in every sign language community, whose ability to create enjoyable, valued language art forms is recognised by other community members. In this section, we will focus principally on the history of creative sign language in the Brazilian deaf community because it is the one that we know best, but we refer to other national deaf communities and we expect readers to find parallels in any nation or deaf community, including their own. For example, for the story of another country's sign language art movement, we highly recommend Nathan Lerner and Feigel's (2009) video documentary *The Heart of the Hydrogen Jukebox* about American Sign Language (ASL) poetry in the twentieth century.

In the following paragraphs, we provide a short introduction to the long history of Brazilian deaf artists and deaf literature, to show the wide range of artistic skills of members of the deaf community. Rich materials document the history of Libras literature (Mourão 2016; Rocha 2008), many of which are informal records, some archived and some almost forgotten, dating back to the foundation of Instituto Nacional de Educação de Surdos (INES), the national school for the deaf in Rio de Janeiro, in 1857.

## Face-to-Face Encounters with Sign Language Literature

Deaf children from all over the country boarded at INES and shared cultural and language experiences. It is well known that school is a key source of most people's language lore (Opie & Opie 1959) and we may say that INES created the roots of Brazilian deaf folklore. The INES graduates returned to their hometowns and shared what they had learned, at their local deaf clubs and at regional artistic events. Records from deaf schools and those of their graduates provide material for academic study, and for deaf children in schools and adults in the deaf community to understand their history, including their literary heritage. Rich records of artistic endeavours have already revealed a hitherto undocumented history of Libras (Rocha 2008). It is important that we collect more material from regions across the country, for researchers worldwide to study documents that shed more light on the literary and artistic history of their deaf communities.

Although most deaf people are born into hearing families, the few families where deaf parents have deaf children are crucial for passing deaf folklore down through the generations (Ladd 2002; Lane et al. 1996). Mourão (2016) reports that the Libras artist Rimar Segala grew up in a deaf family and encountered creative sign language and deaf literature in the form of theatre and storytelling among other deaf families and in the deaf clubs in São Paulo, long before it became a recognised term in academic circles and before it was taught in Libras Studies courses.

Deaf community cultural events have provided important opportunities for sharing and perpetuating sign language creativity. In the past, deaf adults travelled to meet other deaf people face to face at deaf club events and at sports competitions at local, interstate, and international levels. At all these events, people told new stories, poems, and jokes, or performed theatrical sketches which the participants then passed on within their local deaf communities. Bahan (2006) has described how these informal social encounters at sporting events included storytelling and formed part of the face-to-face folkloric tradition of deaf literature in the USA. Charles Krauel's film footage of deaf Americans' social events from the 1920s to 1950s includes several examples of people performing language skits, chants, or stories, while their friends look on (Supalla 1994). Similarly, in Brazil, Strobel (2013) reports that deaf arts of all forms developed through these face-to-face contacts across states within the country.

With the imposition of oralist education methods after the congress of Milan in 1880, institutional support for sign languages and their art forms stopped in schools for deaf children around the world. At INES, the roots of Brazilian deaf folklore were severed, as Libras was repressed. Although we know that it continued, both in schools (including INES) and in deaf associations, we have no clear records of it during most of the twentieth century. The growing recognition of the status of sign languages following the linguistic research of William Stokoe and others in the USA and pioneering researchers in Brazil, such as Lucinda Ferreira Brito and Ronice Müller de Quadros, contributed to the legal recognition of Libras in the Libras Law of 2002. This law's enacting decree in 2005 led to development of Libras teaching, discussion of language, linguistics and culture in Libras, and the establishment of the first Libras Studies Undergraduate Course ('Letras Libras') at UFSC, the Federal University of Santa Catarina, in 2006. This course, offered nationwide through eleven regional hubs, trained over 1,500 students (almost all deaf) and, importantly for creative sign language, included modules on sign language literature, taught by Professor Lodenir Karnopp.

As in many countries, despite the relatively recent 'discovery' of deaf literature by the academy, members of the Brazilian deaf community have known about deaf theatre, deaf jokes, caricatures, and humorous pieces for many years, having learned about them, as we mentioned earlier, while at INES or when attending deaf clubs or sporting events. The students brought their knowledge of deaf folklore to these first Deaf Literature courses in the Libras Studies degree program. It was an unprecedented opportunity for stimulating interest in Libras literature within the deaf community at a national level. The materials used in these early courses had a huge impact on general awareness of deaf literature within the deaf community.

Researchers have frequently noted the importance of deaf folklore for sign language art forms in the deaf community (see, for example, Peters 2000; Carmel 1996; Rutherford 1993; Frishberg 1988). Folklore is a way of expressing the traditions and experience of a particular group. This knowledge is often passed to new generations through language and is transmitted face to face rather than in formal education (Dundes 1965). Deaf folklore generally is concerned with deaf world knowledge and the experience of members of the deaf community (Bahan 1994), and this may be expressed especially in the marked forms of aesthetic signing valued by deaf people. Carmel (1996) uses the term Signlore for deaf folklore that focuses on language. There is a common understanding (Taylor 1948) that literature, being a predominantly written art form is more refined and erudite, practised by educated members of the community, while folklore, being predominantly unwritten, has a lower status, often being termed 'popular'. This attitude stems primarily from a general idea that written creative language is superior to unwritten forms (Hutcheon 2012). However, in many cultures, especially those without a strong written tradition, folklore is indistinguishable from literature and literature contains many elements borrowed from folklore. Within the deaf community, the long tradition of deaf folkloric sign language art forms gives them a highly valued status (Peters 2000; Rutherford 1993).

Sutton-Spence and Quadros (2005) showed that creative sign language has its roots in everyday communicative signing but that it has its own artistic characteristics. In a comparison of two sign language poems, one Brazilian and one British, about the national identity of deaf people (*Brazilian Flag* in Libras by Nelson Pimenta and *Three Queens* in British Sign Language (BSL) by Paul Scott), they identified elements that had their roots in deaf community folklore, but which had become incorporated into sign language poetry. It could be said that the creative sign language produced in Libras before the inception of the Libras Studies courses can be termed deaf folklore but academic interest in it, with critical and codifying approaches as it is increasingly taught formally, began a phase of deaf literature. As study of deaflore moved into academia and formal education, its status grew, artists increasingly recorded their work, and developed a more critical understanding and awareness of the work they composed and performed. Mourão (2016) reports that many deaf Libras artists today did not originally see their work as literature but have come to see it as such since its incorporation in the academic curriculum. Heidi Rose (1992) has offered another perspective – that the advent of video led to ASL literature because it allowed for the easy recording, storage, distribution, and analysis of sign language performances. The two developments of video and academic studies of sign language literature may not be unrelated.

Deaf artists have long performed at their local deaf clubs, but few were known more widely. Before the development of easily accessible video technology in the late twentieth century (Krentz 2006; Rose 1992) and the boom in internet video technology in the twenty-first century (Schallenberger 2010), the only opportunities for their work to become better known were at large events such as at the annual conference held at INES in Rio de Janeiro, and other occasional festivals of deaf art and culture, such as those held in the big cities of São Paulo in the south-east[3] and Porto Alegre in the south.[4] However, these festivals were occasional, one-off events. The Deaf Folklore Festival series at UFSC is an attempt to create a regular festival, holding events biennially since 2014. This concept has spread nationally and there are regular festivals in Brasília in the central west and Recife in the north-east of the country. These Brazilian festivals of creative sign language have links with those in other countries such as France, Chile, and South Africa.[5]

All these festivals encourage artists and their audiences to share in new ideas and provide more material to develop their own art forms nationally, with more records of the literary performances (Sutton-Spence et al. 2016). The French connection with the world's largest and arguably most important deaf artistic performance event, Clin d'Oeil, held biennially in Reims since 2003, has been especially important for creative sign language internationally. At Clin d'Oeil, deaf artists and their audiences meet to see high-quality, often groundbreaking and pioneering sign language performances from around the world, in theatre, film, dance, clowning, storytelling, poetry, and other performance genres.[6] Libras artists have played an increasing part of this international sharing and development since Brazil was showcased as Clin d'Oeil's invited nation in 2017.

Although technological advances and the social isolation caused by the 2020–1 Covid pandemic have reduced the emphasis on live performances, leading to more recorded pieces distributed through the internet, the importance of continued face-to-face events cannot be overstated.

## Generations of Deaf Artists

Sign language artists are made, not born. They may have a particular aptitude for language creativity and performance, but they are the product of their experience and their knowledge of creative language learned from the deaf community. To

---

[3] Encontro de Arte e Cultura Surda, 2003, in São Paulo.
[4] Festival Brasileira de Cultura surda, 2011, in Porto Alegre
[5] SociGo arranges artistic events in South African Sign Language, such as Hands Fest in 2018. www.socigo.org.za/2018-hands-festival.html.
[6] See, for example, www.clin-doeil.eu/.

understand the history of creative sign language, we need to trace the history of the artists who produce it and their experiences and influences.

The documentary *The Heart of the Hydrogen Jukebox* (Nathan Lerner & Feigel 2009) traces the timeline of deaf American sign language artists from the 1940s and their influences, documenting the individual lives of deaf artists and the ways in which these contributed to their styles of ASL signing, theatre, and storytelling that formed the collective concept of ASL poetry by the 1990s. This documentary inspired research along similar lines of artistic generations in Brazil (Sutton-Spence et al. 2017). It rapidly became clear that, as in the USA, the development of Libras literature arose from the communal artistic environment of deaf Brazilian artists and their interaction. (A similar pattern can be seen in the influences on deaf sign language artists in the United Kingdom (Sutton-Spence 2020) and France (L'Huillier & Liennel 2019[7]) and we suspect that it holds true in many countries.)

An important influence on a nation's sign language literature is that of artists in deaf communities in other countries. The exchange of ideas, skills, and training has been as important in Brazil as it has been in other countries. In the USA, despite a long folkloric tradition of creative signing in ASL, the formation of the National Theater of the Deaf (NTD) in 1967 spurred on new experiments in artistic and poetic ASL. The Brazilian Carlos Goes travelled to the USA to study deaf theatre in the 1990s, where he was influenced by the American actor from NTD, Bernard Bragg. On his return to Brazil, Carlos Goes passed on his new knowledge to his home deaf community, including the young Nelson Pimenta Castro, who later also travelled to the USA to study with NTD. When he returned, he published (in 1999) a highly influential DVD *Literatura em LSB* ('Literature in LSB[8]') of fables, stories, and metaphorical pieces adapted from what he had learned in the USA. His poem *Brazilian Flag*[9] had a great impact on Brazilian deaf people, for whom the Brazilian national anthem, with its unusual literary style, was hard to understand.[10] His description of the meaning behind the national flag made it accessible to the deaf community, appealing to their own sense of national cultural and linguistic identity. The interest in Libras poetry and storytelling inspired by the DVD led Nelson Pimenta to give workshops and training in deaf clubs and schools, travelling

---

[7] www.canal-u.tv/chaines/cnrspouchet/entretiens-du-laboratoire-poetique-pour-la-gazette-poetique-et-sociale/le.
[8] LSB is the acronym from Língua de Sinais Brasileira, Brazilian Sign Language, a term that is now used less than the term Libras, which we use here.
[9] In Portuguese, *Bandeira Brasileira*, versions of which can be found through a simple internet search.
[10] The lyrics of the Brazilian national anthem are markedly erudite, using arcane vocabulary and grammatical forms that are a challenge to many citizens, not only members of the deaf community.

with deaf theatre groups to show the Brazilian deaf community artistic sign language that appealed to their own sense of deaf identity. From his work in theatre and poetry, the third generation of Libras artists emerged, and the process continued as they passed on their skills, knowledge, and styles. Perhaps we are now on the fifth generation and, as Mourão (2016) observed, it will continue as deaf people pass on their own creative knowledge, blending it with traditions and knowledge of other members of the deaf community.

Where deaf artists have moved to work within the higher education system, formal teaching at undergraduate level has helped develop new materials, leading to new research, and has trained new creative sign language artists. We have already referred to the fundamental shift in Libras literature that occurred with the nationwide Letras Libras courses of 2006 and 2008. These courses have developed and spread across the country so that deaf literature is taught in at least one federal university in every state in Brazil.

The 'Facebook Libras Poetry Course', first run out of UFSC in 2014, is offered simultaneously to on-site students at the university (in the south of Brazil) and online for deaf people across the country to study by distance learning. There has been great demand for these regular courses, with interest generated partly by the success of the four-day Deaf Folklore Festivals held in 2014 and 2016, at which performances were accompanied by workshops and seminars on different aspects of sign language literature and folklore. Students wanted to extend their knowledge in these year-long courses with weekly meetings. A by-product of these courses is the creation of original materials by the course participants submitted as exercises set during the lessons. These materials have been used in undergraduate teaching, postgraduate research and publication, in creative performances, and in community outreach programmes in the deaf community, including in schools. There are currently few openly and widely available examples of high-quality, original Libras literature to serve as resources for teaching and research, and few texts that teachers can give to students that exemplify the rules and norms of creative sign language, so materials that students created during the 'Facebook' online courses have fed back into subsequent course editions, improving learning year on year.

Graduates of this course have gone on to become sign language professionals, especially teachers. One example is the profile of the Libras poet Victoria Pedroni who took the course as a student while an undergraduate, returned the following year as a teaching assistant, then became one of the teachers on the course, and completed her master's degree on signed poetry duets using materials generated during the course (Pedroni 2021), providing new material for future teaching. Figure 1 shows the three teachers of the course and Figure 2 shows some poetic performances by the students.

**Figure 1** Teachers of the Facebook Libras Poetry course (Left to right: Fernanda Machado, Rachel Sutton-Spence, and Victoria Pedroni)

**Source:** Authors' personal archive.

The edited book by Karnopp, Klein, and Lunardi-Lazzarin (2011) *Cultura Surda na contemporaneidade* [*Contemporary deaf culture*], concerning the production, circulation, and consumption of deaf literature, shows the importance of its visual nature. While research initially focused on illustrated printed books written in Portuguese and in Libras, presented in SignWriting, as well as adaptations of traditional stories known in general Brazilian society for the deaf community, the contributors also acknowledged the increasing role of DVDs and sites such as YouTube in showing the creative, artistic, and cultural richness of deaf literature in Libras. The lack of high-quality material for research into sign language literature has been widely acknowledged among researchers, and a further by-product of the online courses has been that work created has been selected for anthologies of Libras poetry and other literature genres (Machado 2017; Sutton-Spence & Machado 2019).

### Technology and the Evolution of Artistic Productions

Since the first known filmed performance of creative sign language in 1913,[11] technology has dramatically changed how deaf artists produce and disseminate their work. The evolution began slowly, with film, videotape, and DVDs

---

[11] *The Death of Minnehaha*, performed by Mary Williamson Erd. https://commons.wikimedia.org/wiki/File:Death_of_Minnehaha_(1913).webm.

(a)

(b)

**Figure 2** Poetic performances by the students (Sara Amorim, Angela Okumura, and Marcos Marquioto)

**Source:** Authors' personal archive.

(Krentz 2006), but the launch of YouTube in 2005 allowed people with no specialist video or computing knowledge to post videos, and subsequent development in social networking sites means that a signer can upload videos of stories, jokes, sketches, poems, or other presentations quickly and easily. The speed at which these can be shared in these informal spaces attracts increasing audiences of people who have never met the artists. The openness of social networking sites, in conjunction with the increasing accessibility of open seminars, workshops, conferences, and festivals, provides ever more materials to select for inclusion in collections and anthologies. Curating or selecting materials is a way to make this explosion in content more manageable for audiences and researchers of sign language literature.

With the start of the Covid pandemic in early 2020, when many people were confined to their homes, there was an unprecedented boom in creative sign language productions as people expressed their feelings and experiences through forms such as the filmic signed art form Visual Vernacular (VV) (see the section 'Filmic Monologues of VV' later in this Element). The sudden upskilling in online video technology that the pandemic required (using platforms such as Zoom, StreamYard, and Instagram) led to online conferences, festivals, shows,[12] seminars,[13] and workshops that brought deaf people together nationally and world-wide. Crea, a Swedish Theatre Company, for example, hosted online events using International Signing with deaf participants from different countries, watched around the world. Artists and audiences got to know each other and their art forms entirely online, so, for example, two USA-Brazil Slam contests were arranged, with each country hosting one event, and the people who participated had already watched other events online to learn the techniques.

At that time, also, there was a marked increase in the diversity of people producing and disseminating creative sign language, with a surge in interest in material by people identifying as LGBTQ+, as well as by people from different racial and ethnic origins, especially black deaf poetry in Libras.[14] Deaf feminist poets also published more poems addressing women's issues, feminist politics, and deaf women's issues.

Although these positive developments were counterbalanced by lack of context and the loss of face-to-face contact and collective experiences at group festivals, the open, democratic nature of online events broke barriers across age groups, regions, and nationalities. Deaf people took part in events, seminars, and workshops in a range of genres, stimulating creativity among deaf language artists and promoting the status of sign literature and deaf folklore.[15] Compared to the early days described by Bahan and Strobel when deaf people got together occasionally to share stories and other language art, there is still the

---

[12] For example, the 'VV leaders' performance event on 20 April 2020, which brought together VV artists from Brazil, Italy, France, and the USA for a worldwide audience of signers. https://youtu .be/bKJH6ThUG3g.

[13] For example, the Seminars and Workshops held by the online series IEEL, 'Instituto de educação e ensino de Libras' (in English, the Institute for Libras Education and Teaching). https://www .youtube.com/@ieel_libras/featured.

[14] For example, 'Show de poesia de negros surdos' (in English, 'Show of Poetry by Black Deaf People'), on 26 June 2021. https://youtu.be/XD77_Fgdz1U.

[15] Such as 'Vibração Virtual' (in English, 'Virtual vibrations'), part of the online Festival of Deaf Folklore on 12 December 2020. www.youtube.com/live/UwncRt8B3Ks?feature=share.

element of contact and connection between members of the deaf community, but how, where, and when it is done has changed radically.

## Literary Collections and Anthologies in Libras

Another important development made possible by technology is the development of online collections and anthologies.

Corpora of signed literature are limited selections of materials brought together for a particular research objective, whereas a collection is a more open-ended set of materials that can come from a range of sources that can be used for different purposes, especially for teaching and research.

Collections may be organised by individuals to showcase their own works. Technology has allowed deaf artists to produce collections of their own work in film, on VHS, on DVD, and now on the internet. *Gestures* by Dorothy Miles was probably the first collection of ASL poetry, published in 1976, originally distributed on film (deaf clubs could borrow the film from a central distributor, show the film at club room events, and return it) before being transferred to DVD. Collections by other individual artists such as Clayton Valli, Patrick Graybill, and Debbie Rennie in *The Poetry in Motion* series by Sign Media Inc. (1990) and Clayton Valli's *ASL Poetry* (1995) followed on DVD. Many other sign language artists around the world created collections of their work in the 1990s and early twenty-first century (Sutton-Spence & Machado 2019). In Brazil, Nelson Pimenta's DVDs of his poems, stories, and fables in 1999 and 2005 were early examples of technology enabling the distribution of sign language literature of an individual artist. Although they are no longer commercially available, some of these works have been transferred online onto YouTube.

The shift from DVD to online distribution after 2005 has fundamentally changed the face of deaf literature worldwide. Many deaf artists – poets, storytellers, and humourists – post their work on their own social network sites and these are followed by deaf people internationally. There are increasing numbers of online collections of Libras literature that have collated material from different websites, whether original deaf creations or translations and adaptations originating from productions by hearing people. For example, culturasurda.net,[16] founded in 2011 by Hugo Eiji in São Paulo, brings together internet links of productions of various genres which according to the website are 'by, about and for' deaf people in Brazil and other countries. Librando,[17] curated by Michelle Schlemper out of UFSC in Santa Catarina, has similar aims to bring together the diverse publications of original and translated works of deaf literature or about deaf people in Libras (and other sign languages) or in

---

[16] https://culturasurda.net/.     [17] https://librando.paginas.ufsc.br/.

written Portuguese. Both sites have categorised and indexed the materials collected from other sources.

Other collections are of materials created by the hosting institution. Examples among many include those of TV INES,[18] the Art of Signing,[19] and the UFSC online repository of sign language materials.[20] The TV INES collection is an organised collection of stories, poems, and other signed cultural artforms presented and performed by students and teachers at the INES National School for the Deaf. These materials were created for educational purposes, for teachers in other schools where there are deaf children but who have limited resources to download for free and use in their own lessons. The TV INES website is the third technical stage of pioneering production and nationwide distribution to schools of literary materials in Libras that INES has organised. It began with VHS videotapes, followed by transfer to DVD in 2005, and migrated to an online form through the INES YouTube channel. The Rio Branco school for deaf children in São Paulo has a similar collection.[21] There are a range of collections available online of translations of classic stories or of picturebooks for young children translated into Libras by hearing or deaf translators. One example of picturebooks in Libras is Mãos Aventureiras (in English, Adventurous Hands), signed by a deaf translator.[22]

Arte de Sinalizar (in English, The Art of Signing)[23] is a collection of materials filmed at 'open mike' live deaf artistic soirees around the country. Organised by Claudio Mourão at the Federal University of Rio Grande do Sul, it is an example of deaf academics working with the deaf community to create original Libras literature in live, face-to-face settings and store and disseminate it online.

The UFSC online repository[24] stores and manages large amounts of video data, including a collection organised by Fernanda Machado, which includes a poetry anthology, poems from the distance-learning courses for deaf poets already mentioned, recordings from deaf folklore events, and entries for an online glossary of signed literary terms.[25] These, too, are open access and can all be accessed and downloaded for use in teaching and research.

The Libras Portal is a large national repository of materials of many non-literary genres, such as course materials and language corpus recordings, but

---

[18] www.youtube.com/@inesddhct9742.
[19] In Portuguese, Arte de sinalizar, www.ufrgs.br/artedesinalizar/.
[20] https://repositorio.ufsc.br/handle/123456789/172841.
[21] www.youtube.com/playlist?list=PLBCE1E35CE2121DC8..
[22] www.ufrgs.br/maosaventureiras/.    [23] www.ufrgs.br/artedesinalizar/.
[24] https://repositorio.ufsc.br/handle/123456789/176559.
[25] This is another major contribution to the advancement of sign language literature that is made possible by technology. https://glossario.libras.ufsc.br/.

also contains a teaching anthology of Libras literature.[26] The anthology, created between 2018 and 2022, was directed by Ronice Müller de Quadros and edited by us (Rachel and Fernanda) and Anna Luiza Maciel (a deaf poet and actress, as well as researcher). The selection of sixty pieces of work was made by the two deaf artists in the team (Fernanda and Anna Luiza), based on their diversity, relevance, and importance to Libras literature. The pieces were chosen from published DVDs, the online poetry courses offered at UFSC, festival perform-ances, and existing productions on YouTube and other video platforms. The anthology is aimed at teachers and their students, as well as researchers, to provide an easily available set of resource materials.

The anthology is divided into three categories, based on the form of productions and their origins (Bahan 2006; Sutton-Spence & Kaneko 2016): poems, stories of deaf origin, and stories of non-deaf origin. All the poems in the anthology are original deaf creations, and there are no translations of poems from Portuguese (although there is one translation from ASL). Each genre was subdivided into several subgenres, based on research on deaf literature (e.g. Rose 2006; Bahan 2006; Machado 2017) and the editors' own experiences. Subgenres of poems were as follows: constrained forms (e.g. ABC or number poems); dramatic poems, duets, homage, lyric, perspective, deaf music, and haiku. Within the genre of stories of non-deaf origin, we created subgenres of filmic monologues (or VV – see Section 3), Brazilian folklore, and world folklore. Deaf original stories included original fiction in the deaf tradition, original children's stories, personal experience narratives, traditional deaf jokes, and traditional-style deaf theatre sketches.

Unlike in other online collections, the pieces for this primarily teaching anthology were selected for being representative of their genres. Each one was accompanied by detailed headnotes of the piece, with information about the author, the social and historical context, and annotations of each text such as the age group of its target audience, its length and genre, following an adapta-tion of the Protocols for Anthology Introductory Notes suggested by Leitch (2004). We also provided a detailed linguistic analysis highlighting the poetic or other aesthetic devices used in each piece.

The research needed for creation of these headnotes led to a new resource for teachers, students, and researchers of Libras literature, in the form of an online, bilingual book *Libras Literature*[27] with the text in Portuguese and in Libras (Sutton-Spence 2021). It references the works in the anthology and suggests activities for readers, based on these practical examples. Using the works in the anthology, it introduces key concepts about deaf and sign language literature,

---

[26] The anthology is available at https://portal-libras.org, where readers can select 'língua' from the dropdown menu and then 'antologias' from the next menu to reach the materials.

[27] In Portuguese, Literatura em Libras, www.literaturaemlibras.com.

describes the production of signed narratives, outlines the linguistic and aesthetic elements of Libras, and places Libras literature within its social context. It is to these topics of key concepts in creative sign language and the production of signed art forms that we will now turn.

## 2 Aesthetics of Creative Sign Language

In the 2009 documentary on the history of ASL poetry by Nathan Lerner and Feigel, Karen Christie, a deaf poet and educator said 'I can play with language. I can be creative with it. I don't have to . . .just get by with basic communication'. Creative sign language is a chance to play with language and our exploration of it here will show that it is rich, beautiful, ingenious, and often great fun.

Creative sign language brings visual images to the fore. In this section on aesthetics of creative sign language, we will take a broad but fundamentally linguistic approach to it and see how language, performance, and recording and editing techniques create an enjoyable, powerful visual experience that is aesthetically, intellectually, and emotionally satisfying for performers and their audiences. We will draw on examples of performances in several sign languages but focus principally on Libras. However, because our focus is on the visual imagery in creative sign language, we expect that readers unfamiliar with the sign language of the example will still understand the relevant points and will readily find examples in their own national sign languages.

Sign languages can be described as visual-spatial-kinetic languages, produced by 'visible bodily action' (Kendon 2017) that is made mostly above the waist and perceived visually. Sign languages are also highly iconic, meaning that there is usually a recognisable relationship between the visual appearance of the signified (what we are talking about) and the visual appearance of the signifier (the sign we use to talk about it). This iconic relationship is not always especially transparent and in everyday non-creative signing, iconicity is not especially noticeable, but it becomes so in creative sign language, as artists strive to produce powerful visual images, creating 'pictures in the air' (Baldwin 1993).

Visual imagery is important in non-deaf literature, too. The worldwide Concrete Poetry movement in the 1950s and 1960s used written words creatively to draw readers' attention to the visual form of the words. As Pedro Reis (1998) explains, readers were invited to look *at* the written words, instead of looking *through* them to the meaning behind them. This drive for visual imagery in modern poetry, also the aim of the Beat poets such as Allen Ginsberg, had a powerful influence on sign language poets in the USA in the 1980s. Peter Cook, a leading ASL poet, said:

> The beat poets were after images, trying to find the words to convey strong pictures, and not rely on the sounds to do the work for them, but the right word

itself. It was like a tapestry of images and words and knowledge that they were weaving all together. I think what we're doing is the same – taking the images we see and embodying them with signs or movements, weaving them together in a parallel way, just like the beats did. (Peter Cook in Nathan Lerner & Feigel 2009, 1:14:38)

We understand, then, that in creative sign language, we are simultaneously looking *at* the signs and looking *through* them to their meaning.

## The Visual Nature of Signs

Sign language artists create their work using the body articulators they have at their disposal: the hands, arms, torso, neck-head, face, eyes, and mouth. The hands may be described according to the parameters of their handshape or configuration, their place of articulation and their movement, as well as orientation of the fingers and palm and whether the arm is used meaningfully or not. For our purposes of exploring creative sign language, we can say that the 'visible bodily actions' made by these articulators create and portray meaning visually in three basic ways: through conventional signs, classifier signs (also termed transfer of form or situation), and embodiment (also widely termed constructed action or transfer of person).[28] (For more details on these, see more general texts by Johnston and Schembri (2007) and Sutton-Spence and Woll (1999). See also Aarons and Morgan (2003), Dudis (2007), Cuxac and Sallandre (2007), Metzger (1995), Quinto-Pozos (2007), Ferrara and Johnston (2014), and Cormier and Smith (2014)).

Of the three basic ways, conventionalised vocabulary signs contain the most propositional content in any sign language. They are most analogous to vocabulary words in spoken languages and are primarily articulated by the hands. Although most signs have some sort of iconic link between the form of a sign and the form of its referent, when signers use vocabulary items, they do not usually have a specific 'illustrative intent' (Cuxac & Sallandre 2007) but simply use them to identify a referent. In creative sign language, conventionalised vocabulary signs are often crucial for giving information that identifies the referent. The specific signs may be chosen for aesthetic reasons in creative signing, but their iconicity is usually less important than their physical form (e.g. a poet may wish to use a sign with a particular handshape) or simply for its

---

[28] These devices for signing have been termed many things but we use these terms here because within the Brazilian Sign Language community they are usually called classifiers and embodiment (classificadores and incorporação). The term 'classifier signs', especially, in sign languages has been problematised, for example by Schembri (2003), but they are commonly used in sign linguistic publications and so we will maintain them here.

(a)  (b)  (c)

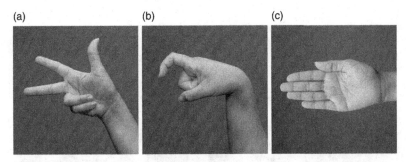

**Figure 3** Whole entity classifier handshapes to show a bicycle in ASL, Libras, and BSL

**Source:** Created by the authors.

meaning.[29] Classifiers and constructed actions through embodiment, however, are highly iconic structures (to use the term by Cuxac 2000) and are used when signers deliberately intend to emphasise the visual appearance of something.

Classifier signs, or transfers of form or situation, are particularly used to show the shape or form of something and its location, orientation, and manner of movement through space. While conventional vocabulary signs *name* and identify the referent, classifier signs *show* it, as the hand stands for the referent itself. In entity classifiers (or transfers of situation), the handshape shows the shape, size, or appearance of the referent under discussion, and it is usually iconic, although conventionalised in different languages. For example, the classifier handshape for a bicycle is different in ASL, Libras, and BSL. The ASL classifier shows the general shape of a vehicle, the Libras handshape focuses on the round wheel of the bicycle, and the BSL handshape emphasises its largely two-dimensional form (see Figure 3).

Whatever the handshape that is used, however, the hand then moves iconic-ally or is simply located in an iconically meaningful place. If the bicycle moves left to right, the hand in that handshape moves analogously left to right; if the bike goes right to left, the hand moves right to left.

In embodiment or transfer of person, the signer takes on the role of the referent, and effectively 'becomes' it by transferring or mapping the body of the referent onto their own body. When signers embody a human character, they show the emotions and behaviour of that character. If the signer raises a hand, it means that the character raised a hand and if, for example, they do it cautiously, the articulators will show the cautiousness. Signers can also embody non-humans.

---

[29] That said, creative signers can reactivate the dormant iconicity in conventional signs and treat them again as though they had illustrative intent, and the signs can be manipulated creatively to further push the boundaries of the language.

(a)

(b)

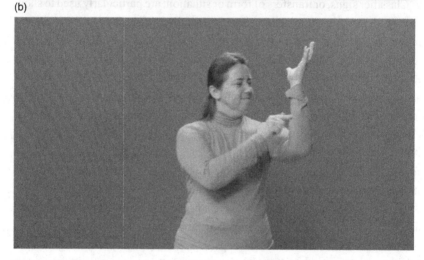

**Figure 4** Options for visual portrayal of a woodpecker – by embodiment and use
of classifiers with embodiment

**Source:** Based on Panara 1984, modelled by Fernanda Machado, and Lohn 2020 from
*The Animals* (*numbers*).

When the signers' human body does not have the parts necessary to map onto the
referent, the hands can represent them. Thus, for example, in Robert Panara's
classic 1984 performance of haiku poems translated into ASL, he incorporated
a woodpecker. In Figure 4 (a), we can see that the human body and head represent
the woodpecker's body and head. However, as humans have neither a beak nor

a tail, the hands are placed on the face and back, analogous to where they would be on the bird, to represent the beak and tail.[30]

Classifier signs may be part of the narration of facts, merely showing the referent's form, location, and movement, but many classifiers are used simultaneously with embodiment, especially in creative sign language. The arms and hands produce the classifier, while the body, head, and articulators on the face show embodiment. In the example of a woodpecker here by Juliana Lohn in *The Animals (numbers)*,[31] the hand configuration of the right hand is a classifier that represents the bird's head, and the forearm is its body, while the left hand and forearm make the classifier handshape for the tree against which the woodpecker pecks (the wood that Panara's incorporated woodpecker pecks is not shown but easily imagined by the audience). Her own head and body embodying the bird mirror the movement of the classifier (see Figure 4 (b)).

Given the highly visual, non-conventional nature of a lot of aesthetic, creative signing, it might be reasonable to ask if it is part of a named sign language at all, or if it is acting or gesture, or something else. The question raises many important points about the nature of language and performance and sign language literature. The academic linguistic study of creative sign language began in the 1970s with Klima and Bellugi's pioneering work on what they termed 'heightened uses of ASL' or 'art sign' (1979, p. 140). This led to a chapter entitled 'Poetry and song in a language without sound' in their 1979 classic *The Signs of Language*. They distinguished internal poetic structure from external poetic structure. Internal poetic structure was 'constituted from elements completely internal to the linguistic system proper (words in spoken language, signs in ASL)' (p 341) and external poetic structure was the part in which 'the basic devices include creating a balance between the two hands, creating and maintaining a flow of movement between signs and manipulating the parameters of the signs' (p.341). Thus, they focused on the choice of signs (internal poetic structure) and how they are presented (external poetic structure).

This division of internal structure as being about language and external structure as being about performance is undeniably useful for describing creative sign language. However, it is difficult, possibly fruitless, and perhaps ultimately unhelpful, to make a division between what is 'completely internal to the linguistic system proper' and what is not. One of the benefits of studying creative sign language has been its contribution in recent years to the questions of what is – and what is not – sign language or a sign language. Proponents of

---

[30] From Robert Panara's untitled ASL haiku which begins 'Ah! My forest hut' at 19:50 in https://youtu.be/faJfH8yUECU.

[31] In Portuguese, *Os Animais (números)* at 00:33 in https://vimeo.com/showcase/6241328/video/348189766.

translanguaging argue that users of any language draw upon the total of their communicative resources when they are interacting with others. Kusters et al. (2017) have argued convincingly that translanguaging allows signers to use freely resources that previous sign linguistic thinking has often referred to as 'gesture' outside the closed system of a given language. Kusters and Sahasrabudhe (2018) show that the everyday language ideologies of deaf people's understanding of a language-gesture distinction is different from that of academic language ideologies.

This difference has been expressed by deaf people for decades. Stewart's (1990) definition of what ASL encompasses exemplifies a different approach to the definition of deaf signing from what was widely understood within linguistic research at the time:

> The reality is that most deaf folks have had to use whatever was at hand at the time, theory be damned, including SEE-1, SEE-2, SEE Heinz 57, Siglish, the Rochester method, Cued Speech, gestures, . . . eye-blinking, face twitching, head nodding, ear wiggling, and just about anything else that might possibly help to bridge the vast gulf that normally separates us deaf people from one another. (1990, p. 118)

As more linguists question the reality of a closed system of any language, creative sign language shows the potential of signers to use a range of devices drawing on their repertoire of visual communication. Thus, in our discussion of creative sign language, we are not overly concerned with the question 'is this part of a language?' Rather, we accept as a positive fact that deaf artists fluent in any sign language draw on all their available resources in the creation and performance of their visual work.

## Linguistic and Performance Features

### *Foregrounding Language – 'It's how you say it'*

Creative language deviates from everyday language and even appears to break its rules. This deviation brings language to the foreground so that we notice it. It calls attention to itself by being unexpected because the surprising way that something is expressed stands out and creates an aesthetic effect in the audience.

Foregrounded language is at the foundation of sign language literature and its performance. Language artists can create foregrounding in two different but often complementing ways. In *parallelism* or *obtrusive regularity*, existing elements that are already used in non-creative everyday language are used creatively, often by repeating them so often that they stand out. In *deviance* or *obtrusive irregularity*, artists create new possibilities by going beyond established language norms and use forms that are not in the language (or, at least, not yet) (Leech 1969). In summary, obtrusively regular language is odd because it uses something that is part of the language too often to be normal; obtrusively irregular language is odd because it breaks the language rules in some way, doing something that the language is not expected to do. We see this in any creative language, whether spoken, written, or signed, but the high meta-linguistic awareness among signers about their languages is important, given the long history of disparaging views of sign languages as less than languages.

Repetition is part of the *obtrusive regularity* that leads to foregrounding and is the basis for a wide range of aesthetic effects in creative language. For example, using an ordinary word or sign with extraordinary frequency in creative language will create an effect of obtrusive regularity. So may repeating elements at the phonemic (or sub-sign) level, for example, repeating the same handshape in different signs, or the same movement but with different hand-shapes or in different locations. The same movement path could be made repeatedly in different directions, at different speeds, or with different emphasis. Alternatively, the same sign could be repeated but with different handshapes or in different locations or with a different speed, direction, or size of movement. Any of these repetitions, once they are made beyond what is considered 'normal', will foreground the language and, if used with deliberate artistic intent, can be part of the visual aesthetics of a creative or literary work.

In *obtrusively irregular* sign language creativity, we may see a sign with the 'wrong' handshape or even with a handshape that is not part of the language's normal phonemic system. The deviant sign could be articulated in an unex-pected 'wrong' place or made with the 'wrong' movement. The deviance may be in meaning as well as in form. The artist may, for example, use a sign that normally means one thing but means something different in the creative context. Audiences who are used to the norms of their literature will know when to look for another meaning behind the apparent one, as for example, in metaphor.

When we explore the different types of aesthetic sign language, we will see that this linguistic creativity leads to some sort of literary effect, adding signifi-cance in some way.

## Performance

Heidi Rose (1992) observed that the performance of sign language literature has an acknowledged text, defined as 'the original words of an author', and a performed text that includes 'all aspects of articulation, gesticulation and mise-en-scene' (1992, p. 23). Most creative sign language is performed (apart from written sign language literature, which we discuss in Section 3), so it is important to address the question of what is added to the text by the performer.

We may divide performance elements into those that are internal to the text (e.g. the way that an embodied character is portrayed) and those that are external to it (e.g. how the performer engages with the audience).

Analyses of written texts usually do not consider how they are performed, apart from dramatic scripts. However, the performance even of non-dramatic texts influences the way they are received, especially when a story is read aloud, rather than read silently. When someone tells a story in spoken languages, there is a major performance element.

Folkloric pieces such as traditional stories, rhymes, and jokes have specific structures and plots but do not have a fixed text and are not attributed to any one author. This was the case in sign languages before technology allowed recordings of creative pieces and their easy widespread distribution. Cynthia Peters (2000) has suggested that recorded versions of a definitive performance come to be seen as 'the' performance, which may be regarded as 'the' text. When other people perform this piece, they may bring their own performance to it, maintaining certain elements and changing others. Comparing two performances of a piece, either by the same person or by different people, can show us what elements the performers consider to be performance and what is text.

When considering sign language performances, it is not always clear if we are seeing a poem, narrative story, or theatrical piece. Traditional divisions between narrative and drama are based on the idea that a narrative includes the role of a narrator who tells the story, while in a dramatic piece the actor acts out the story and presents it directly. In creative sign language, however, we know that cinematic signing of narratives or poems, for example, is grammatically similar to film, which rarely has a narrator. Thus, when we talk about the roles of narrator and characters, it is not always clear what or who the artist's body represents in a performance. This is particularly the case when we are thinking about '1st person narratives'. When the signer presents a scene from the character's viewpoint, their body shows the 'I' of the character, not the 'I' of the narrator, and neither of these is necessarily the 'I' of the artist.

We will now consider several devices linked to ways in which sign language artists can manipulate the language creatively: selection of handshapes and their obtrusively regular use; choice of handshape in new 'deviant', obtrusively irregular classifier signs; the use of space and symmetry in signs to create highly visual images; the rhythm and speed of movement of the signs; non-manual elements of gaze, facial expression, and body movement; direct presentation of humans and of non-humans through embodiment and anthropomorphism; filmic signing with a different grammar from that used in everyday signing. Some of these aspects are more related to the 'text' and some to the 'performance', but taken together, they create the powerful impacts of creative signing.

## Handshape

Careful selection of signs with certain handshapes and manipulation of these handshapes foregrounds the language. Repeated use of certain handshapes creates aesthetic effect by obtrusive regularity and unusual handshapes or signs with unexpected handshapes foreground the language through obtrusive irregularity.

In sign language literature, especially in poetry, repetition of handshape is a common device that creates an effect similar to that of rhyme or alliteration in spoken language poetry. Creative sign language, as Ben Bahan has observed (2006), is not isolated from creative discourse in other languages. Sign language artists are educated in and familiar with the broader literary traditions in their country and around the world, and the concept of rhyme in written languages finds a parallel in sign language poems.

Until the 1970s, sign language poetry was usually based on translations of written poetry and its aesthetic form relied principally on rhythm and movement because translating rhyme always presents considerable challenges. In the early 1970s, the pioneering deaf poet Dorothy Miles began composing original poetry in ASL according to poetic principles similar to the ones used in English poems. In a television interview in 1976, she explained, 'I am trying . . . to find ways to use sign language according to the principles of spoken poetry. For example, instead of rhymes like "cat" and "hat", I might use signs like WRONG and WHY, with the same final handshape' (in ASL, both use the 'Y' handshape). The idea of creating aesthetic effect in original (i.e., not translated) sign language poetry by drawing on the structural elements of sign language was an important insight and has since become a foundation of creative signing.

There are various possibilities for repeating handshapes. Creative signers can repeatedly use signs with a specific handshape among other signs, and the repetition is enough to foreground that handshape. They can also alternate between two different handshapes, contrasting two ideas. They can even use a single handshape throughout. As examples, we will describe two very different pieces that use a single 'Y' handshape: one a humorous narrative aimed at children and the other a haiku poem.

Every sign in the Libras children's story *The Deaf Cow in High Heels*[32] by Marina Teles (2019) is made using the 'Y' handshape (with the thumb and little finger extended from a closed hand). This humorous story, derived from an idea by Smith and Jacobowitz (2006), unites two unremarkable signs in a ludicrous, incongruous way. The Libras signs for 'cow' and 'walk-in-high-heels' both use the Y handshape, and neither is intrinsically amusing, but putting them together because of their shared handshape generates a silly scenario that children (and

---

[32] *A Vaca surda de salto alto* in Portuguese. https://vimeo.com/356033857/9e5d448ab6.

**Figure 5** Same handshapes in two signs. The left hand signs the mobile phone, while the right hand signs 'Hello', both with the Y handshape

**Source:** https://vimeo.com/showcase/6241328/video/356033857.

adults) enjoy. In the story, the cow is shown with fluttering eyelashes and long floppy ears, as she chews the cud and sets off walking in her high heels. She looks up at an aeroplane overhead and falls over. She gets up and carries on walking as her mobile phone vibrates. She answers it, signing 'Hello!' (it is a video call because she is a deaf cow) and falls over again. She gets up again, walking on her high heels, despite being very large and finally stands proudly in the high heels, which slide apart in the mud and she falls for a third time. She gets up crossly and raises her head with her horns high.

Using the same handshape for every sign in the story creates a strong aesthetic effect through obtrusive regularity because it would be highly unusual in everyday signing. It is also effective because of obtrusively irregular signs where the storyteller has manipulated the handshape to fit the constraints of the story. The Libras sign 'Hello!' does not use the Y handshape (although the correct handshape is similar, with the little finger extended) but the cow makes it with the Y, using the correct movement at the correct location to make perfect sense (see Figure 5).

The classifier sign for long floppy cow's ears would not normally use the Y handshape, but the orientation, location, and movement of the sign means that we know they are her ears. Eyelashes would normally be signed with all the fingers open, not just the thumb and little finger, as we see here, but again, the context of location and movement and the non-manual elements mean it is easily understood. The effect of breaking the language rules to fit the single-handshape rule is doubly obtrusive and remarkably funny (see Figure 6).

**Figure 6** The cow's dainty eyelashes, signed with the Y handshape
**Source:** https://vimeo.com/showcase/6241328/video/356033857.

All the signs in the Libras haiku poem *Calling the Cattle*[33] by João Raphael Bertoncelli (2019) also use the 'Y' handshape. In central Brazil, drovers have traditionally blown on an unusually long 'berrante' horn to call their cattle across long distances. In this very short poem, a cattle drover on a horse unslings his berrante and blows on it, and a bullock raises its head in response.

The first three manual signs show the horse's reins, the strap that holds the horn slung over the drover's shoulder and finally the horn that the drover blows. For these three signs, the two hands are joined at the point of contact of the tip of the little finger and the tip of the thumb (this is a highly irregular point of contact. There are no established Libras signs that use it). The berrante horn is remarkably long[34] and the 'Y' hand configuration, with the thumb and index finger extended as far from the other fingers as possible, is already one of the longest handshapes possible in Libras (and the other closed fingers make it look even longer). Joining this long handshape end to end makes these signs markedly long (in size, not time). The final sign shifts the poem's view from the drover to the bullock. The two hands separate to show the horns on both sides of the animal's head. The contrast in size between the signs is dramatic, but the handshape is the same (see Figure 7).

None of the signs related to the drover is an existing sign in Libras vocabulary. They have all been created to show the length of the reins, of the strap holding the horn, and of the horn itself. The only sign that is part of existing sign language vocabulary is the sign for 'cow' or 'bullock' that is made with the Y handshape.

---

[33] *Chamar Boi* in Portuguese, https://repositorio.ufsc.br/handle/123456789/200847.
[34] Readers unfamiliar with the berrante horn can easily find images by searching on the internet.

(a)                                    (b)

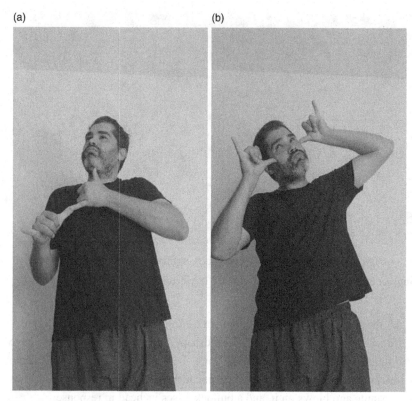

**Figure 7** João Raphael Bertoncelli signing blowing the berrante horn and the
bullock looking up

**Source:** https://repositorio.ufsc.br/handle/123456789/200847.

Producing all the signs in the first part of the poem with the Y handshape links the
drover firmly with the idea of the cattle.

Handshapes can also carry metaphorical meaning, separate from the meaning
of the sign. For example, Kaneko (2008) showed that 'clawed' handshapes are far
more common in BSL signs that have negative connotations in contrast to
handshapes with straight fingers that usually carry more positive meaning.
Carvalho (2018) showed this is also the case in Libras. Thus, repeated handshapes
with bent or 'clawed' fingers can create negative meaning within a story or poem.
Fernanda Machado's poem *Where Food Comes From*[35] uses only signs with bent
or 'clawed' fingers for the poor, oppressed farm labourer and only signs with open
straight fingers for the rich, privileged city-dweller (See Figure 13).

We will see (in the next section) in the discussion of different genres of
creative sign language that different forms of deaf literature use handshape as

---

[35] In Portuguese, *Como veio alimentação*. https://youtu.be/nMOTYprbYoY.

**Figure 8** André Conceição's novel classifier handshape, showing two adults and a child walking side by side

**Source:** https://vimeo.com/267272296/e685ec89f9.

their base, such as those that follow a written alphabet (often termed 'ABC genres', in sign languages whose manual alphabets begin that way), single handshape, and number games of the sign language traditions.

### Established and Novel Classifier Handshapes

Sign language artists aim to produce powerful visual images in their performances. When the way to create the images is novel and unexpected, the aesthetic language stands out even more than when conventional signs are used. For example, the handshapes of most entity classifier signs are conventionalised within a given sign language, but when the classifier handshape is novel, its creativity provides extra impact. In *Tree* by André Luiz Conceição,[36] a small child fetches two adults to see a tree. Normally, there is no deliberate attempt to link the height of the person represented in the classifier handshape to the length of the fingers on the hand. One person is conventionally shown by the index finger; two people by the index and middle fingers; and three people by the index, middle, and ring fingers. However, André uses the latent iconicity in the length of the fingers to produce the novel classifier in Figure 8 so that the little finger represents the child alongside the two adults. This handshape is not part of the conventionalised phonemic repertoire of Libras and is not seen in any Libras signs, but its meaning is completely transparent in this context.

---

[36] *Árvore* in Portuguese, https://vimeo.com/267272296/e685ec89f9. This poem was inspired by the BSL poem *Tree* by Paul Scott, https://youtu.be/TaQIdovqsFg.

**Figure 9** Fernanda Machado's novel classifier handshape showing a jaguar
walking while roaring

**Source:** https://youtu.be/4UBwn9242gA.

Fernanda Machado's piece *Saci*[37] presents a jaguar that comes to sleep under
the Saci's tree. The classifier handshape representing a whole animal such as
a big cat like a jaguar would conventionally focus on the animal's legs. In this
poem, the animal is shown entirely by its roaring jaws (see Figure 9).

## Use of Space and Symmetry

Signers inhabit their signing space and can move within it in three dimensions.
Because the hands and body exist in space, all signs must be articulated in space,
even those with no meaningful movement, but the planned use of space in
creative sign language is essential. As well as smooth descriptions of a static
image, sign language artists place and move classifier signs to show action –
where objects or characters are and how they move.

When we watch good storytelling, we see that signs are placed and moved to
produce clear, entertaining visual images for the audience. Importantly, skilled
sign language artists use the whole of the signing space, moving their hands and
bodies in signs in all planes (left to right, front to back, and up and down). Not
only do the hands move in this space, but the eyes, head, and trunk move and are
directed to different parts of the space.

---

[37] A Saci is a Brazilian folklore character who is a mischievous sprite. The piece is at https://youtu
   .be/4UBwn9242gA.

Klima and Bellugi's pioneering study of art sign in the 1970s identified a tendency to reduce the transition movement between signs. This is partly because the careful placement of signs is visually relaxing and enjoyable. If we observe descriptions of the appearance of a character at the start of a signed story, we often see the signs moving steadily in one direction (usually downwards), that the eyes can easily follow, creating a smooth impression. For example, Marina Teles' description of an ant in *The Deaf Brazilian Indian Ant*[38] (a story aimed at young children) starts with the sign for an ant (on the top of her head; see Figure 10 (a)) and then shows its appearance by detailing the eyes, mouth, and legs, in that order (see Figure 10 (b) to (d)). Had the signer shown the sign on the head, then the legs, mouth, and eyes, the movements between signs would have been greater and the audience's gaze would track far less smoothly.

In practice, this often means that the place where one sign ends is the place where the next sign starts. This obtrusively smooth transition becomes even more noticeable when the handshape of the following sign is the same as the previous one. Morphing one sign into another is especially common in poetry, where signers are trying to create a smooth visual rhythm with the minimum of disruption to the flow of signs.

The calm impression given in *Calling the Cattle* by João Raphael Bertoncelli partly stems from the careful morphing transition with minimal movement between the signs. The creative signs showing the horse's reins, the strap holding the berrante horn, and the horn itself, all blend into each other. The handshape and arrangement of the hands is the same for all three sign units, and each new sign starts where the last one ends, so the only difference is in the movement and orientation of the hands.

We know that storytellers use space to show where objects or characters are and how they move. This use of space changes depending on the viewpoint that is presented. For example, the same scene can be presented from the viewpoints of people at different places (above and below, to the left and right, or close and distant), meaning that the signs are also placed to represent the different viewpoints. Audiences accustomed to these changes in perspective enjoy the richness of images presented, although as with literacy in any language, audiences need to learn how to interpret the meaning of the images. This is one reason why non-signers who do not know these strategies struggle to follow stories that are highly iconic.

In Figure 11, from Nelson Pimenta's telling of the Aesop's Fable *The Frog and the Ox,*[39] we see viewpoints from two characters in a scene: above and

---

[38] In Portuguese, *A Formiga Indígena Surda*. https://vimeo.com/showcase/6241328/video/355984518.

[39] https://repositorio.ufsc.br/handle/123456789/203681.

(a)

(b)

**Figure 10** Signs articulated in steadily lower locations in Marina Teles' *The Deaf Brazilian Indian Ant*

**Source:** https://vimeo.com/showcase/6241328/video/355984518.

below and to the left and right. The tall and majestic ox looks down and to the left at the small and envious frog, who looks up and to the right at the ox. The use of space in the series of exchanges between the roles of the ox and frog has been likened to camera angle in a film portrayal.

In Gustavo Gusmão's story *Hand Island*,[40] we see an example of two different perspectives of distance – first distant and then close – as waves are shown washing against the island. In the first image, the signer's left hand represents

---

[40] In Portuguese, *A Ilha da Mão*. https://repositorio.ufsc.br/handle/123456789/202024.

(c)

(d)

**Figure 10** (cont.)

(a) (b)

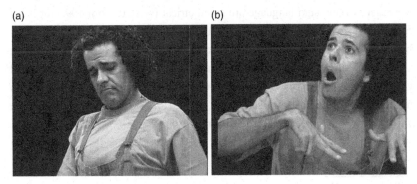

**Figure 11** Nelson Pimenta's frog and ox showing two characters' viewpoints
**Source:** repositorio.ufsc.br/handle/123456789/203681.

the entire island, and the right hand shows the expanse of sea washing up against it, equivalent to an opening distance shot in a film (see Figure 12 (a)). In the second image, signed immediately after the first, the artist's whole body represents the island, and both hands represent the sea washing against it, equivalent to the close-up shot in a film (see Figure 12 (b)).

Signs can also be placed in space with metaphorical meaning. Many cultures use the orientational metaphor (Lakoff & Johnson 1980) that GOOD IS UP. This metaphor can be expressed musically, so that, for example, a descending bass line in music creates a sad impression in listeners and a rising one gives a happier feeling. It is also expressed in language and in English, for example, we see phrases like 'raised self-esteem' to mean 'improved self-esteem' and 'put someone down' to mean assert one's dominance over a person. In creative sign language, we see this spatial metaphor played out directly in space. In Fernanda Machado's *Where Food Comes From*, the signs representing the rich, privileged city-dweller are placed higher than signs for the poor, oppressed agricultural labourer. The poem also uses a second metaphor that signs placed in contrasting parts of space have contrasting meaning. All the signs referring to the labourer are placed on the right and the signs referring to the city-dweller are on the left.[41]

In Figure 13, the raised left hand and fingers and the raised head angled to the left show the powerful city-dweller looking around at delicious food, while the lower right hand and downward-pointing fingers represent the oppressed labourer's plough.

This poem is also an example of careful use of space to create symmetry, which carries aesthetic meaning because in many cultures symmetry symbolises order, balance, and harmony (Weyl 1952). There are several types of symmetry, many of which can be created in signing space. The best-known type is 'reflection', which is mirror-like symmetry. This reflective symmetry, especially left–right symmetry, is very common in creative sign language because the human body is essentially symmetrical on the left and right sides. Most two-handed signs in the vocabulary of any sign language are symmetrical (see Crasborn 1995 for NGT [Sign Language of the Netherlands], Napoli & Wu 2003 for ASL and Sutton-Spence & Kaneko 2007 for BSL), so a symmetrical two-handed sign is not especially aesthetic by itself, but symmetry can be deliberately foregrounded when it is used with obtrusive regularity. Machado (2013) found that many poems in Libras use both hands at the same time, often with the same hand configuration which creates an appreciated sense of symmetry.

---

[41] We should note that sign languages rarely use the widespread metaphor in European languages GOOD IS RIGHT; BAD IS LEFT.

(a)

(b)

**Figure 12** Distance and close-up shots of the sea washing against an island in
Gustavo Gusmão's *Hand Island*

**Source:** https://repositorio.ufsc.br/handle/123456789/202024 (modelled by Fernanda
Machado).

Although reflective symmetry is most commonly left–right across the vertical (or longitudinal) plane, it can also be top–bottom across the horizontal (or
transversal) plane or front–back across a frontal plane. Placing signs across the

**Figure 13** Metaphorical use of space in Fernanda Machado's *Where Food Comes From*, where higher signs are associated with social power and lower signs with lack of social power

**Source:** https://youtu.be/nMOTYprbYoY.

horizontal and frontal planes of symmetry is highly marked (because most signs are symmetrical across the vertical plane), so using these two other planes is especially aesthetically satisfying.

Symmetry also becomes an aesthetic device when every sign is deliberately placed or moved symmetrically. Marina Teles' story of *The Deaf Brazilian Indian Ant*, for example, is deliberately and obtrusively symmetrical, so that the first sign ANT is the only sign in the entire story articulated with one hand. Alternatively, signs that would not naturally be symmetrical are made so, for example, doubling one-handed signs or making the handshapes the same in two-handed signs with different handshapes on each hand.

In rotational (rotating) symmetry, signs that have the same parameters and are in the same plane rotate around a central axis. In translation symmetry, the hands slide in different positions, but we know that if they were together again, they would become symmetrical again. In dilation symmetry, we change the size of one sign relative to another, but all other dimensions remain the same (Machado 2013; Napoli & Wu 2003; Pedroni 2021; Sutton-Spence 2021). All these different types of symmetry occur in the haiku poem *Bonsai* by Gustavo Gusmão (2019).[42]

---

[42] https://repositorio.ufsc.br/handle/123456789/208466.

This poem starts by showing a mighty tree, but when this apparently huge tree is snipped with delicate scissors and placed on a shelf, we understand that it is really a bonsai tree that only imagines it is great. Both hands are held in reflective symmetry as the great tree is described, but the two hands are also moved in a circular pattern around the signing space in rotational and translational symmetry, and move outwards, expanding to give a sense of dilation symmetry. The effect of this repetition and the range of symmetrical structures is to impress the audience with the size of the tree. Symmetry is maintained when there is a sudden shift in contrast from the apparently large tree to the human holding the small pot in his hands. This dilation symmetry of the signs contrasts the large tree and the small pot and is the moment when we come to understand the contrast between the two key ideas in the poem.[43]

When embodying more than one character, signers distinguish them by changes in movement, direction, and posture of the body, head, and gaze, but it is generally expected that creative signing will be performed within the standard signing space. However, as creative signing is often performed standing up, performers can and do move through space, even when telling stories or declaiming poems. This is especially important when the performance is in front of a large audience, for example in Slam poetry, when the artist may move towards the audience to interact more with them. We will see later that the performance use of space is also important in signed duets as one body is located and moves in relation to the other. The real, physical changes in location can be replicated in filmed performances where editing effects can show the signer not always central on the screen.

## *Rhythm and Speed of Movement*

All signing has a natural rhythm and cadence, with stressed and unstressed movements of different signs. This creates a prosodic segmentation of the text at constituent, phrase, and discourse boundaries, making the signing fluent and easy to process and understand (see, for example, Stone 2009). On top of this, however, creative signing may produce effects of obtrusive regularity by imposing on the signing a particular repeated speed, size, or direction of movement (Catteau 2020). It may also disrupt expected rhythms of the underlying language by, for example, adding or altering the timing of pauses, or signing faster or slower than expected. Additionally, sign language artists can supress the natural rhythm of signs. In signed haiku, for example, the neutrality and restraint of sign movement creates an obtrusively subtle and controlled effect.

---

[43] More examples of different types of symmetry can be seen in *Flight over Rio* (in Portuguese *Voo sobre o Rio*) by Fernanda Machado, https://youtu.be/YaAy0cbjU8o.

**Table 1** Six gaze patterns in creative sign language, adapted from Kaneko and Mesch 2013

|  | Direction | Role of poet | Function | Internal/external |
| --- | --- | --- | --- | --- |
| Gaze to audience | Audience/camera | Narrator | Explain, comment | External |
| Character's gaze | Various | Character | Show | Internal |
| Spotlight gaze | On hands | Poetic tool | Highlight, foreground | Internal |
| Reactive gaze | On hands | Observer | Reflect, react | External |
| Panoptic gaze | Various | Poetic tool | Provide whole picture | Internal |
| Prescient gaze | Various | Poetic tool | Foretell | Internal |

## Gaze

The element of gaze is fundamental to the grammar of sign languages, but is also strongly linked to its creative performance, partly because of its role in connecting the performer to the audience and partly because gaze is part of the embodiment of the characters that are directly represented in the creative piece.

Kaneko and Mesch (2013) describe in depth the use of gaze in creative sign language. They highlight six different types of gaze (summarised in the first column of Table 1, an edited version of their table). For each type, they note the direction of the gaze and what role the performer is in at that moment, whether narrator, character, observer, or artist. The authors also identify the function of each gaze type, which can be to engage the audience while the artist addresses them directly, to show the character's gaze directly, to highlight a certain sign, to react to the sign, to extend the meaning of the sign, or to predict the location and something of the meaning of the next sign. The different types of gaze may be specifically used to engage with the audience as part of the performance and are 'external' to the creative piece, or they may be purely internal to its text. Study of the gaze in any creative sign language will reveal the extraordinary complexity of its use.

## Facial Expression, Body Movement

Facial expression and body movement are linked to the identification and creation of characters in embodiment. However, this performance element goes beyond an exact representation of a character's appearance, and both are often exaggerated for performance effect (although, in contrast, marked restraint in facial expression and body movement is also highly effective). To understand how this may be seen as a performance element important for engaging an audience as well as an internal part of the piece, we can note that the ASL artist Stephen Ryan advised (1993, p. 147): 'The exaggeration of facial expression is very significant. An inadequate facial expression is like telling a story in a monotone.'

Relatively little research has been done to date on the role of the rest of the body in signed performance, but there is no doubt that skilled sign language artists involve the whole body in their signing. The position and movement of the head, shoulders, and chest are essential for identifying different characters and for showing how they feel and the way they act and react in the narrative of the piece. Close study of any artistic piece in sign language will show how these body articulators complement the manual signs and facial expression.

## Embodiment and Anthropomorphism

Frequently in our discussion so far, we have referred to the fact that sign language artists embody characters in their performances, through constructed action. Thus, instead of narrating the actions of a character (saying, 'Character N did this'), the signer takes on the role of that character and shows those actions occurring ('I am Character N doing this'). This constructed action is not uncommon during speech, for example when recounting a personal story about being told to tidy our room as a child, we may say 'And my mum was like' and then fall silent while we act out the mother standing firmly, glaring at the untidiness. However, in sign languages, this embodiment is far more common and is essential in good storytelling. Ryan (1993) advised aspiring storytellers to 'Flesh out the characters. Imagine their appearance. Experiment with gestures, mime, signs and facial expression' (p. 146). These aspects are shown through embodiment.

When two or more characters are embodied, they are distinguished by different movements of the body, head, and gaze. For example, facing leftward for one character and rightward for another, or if the two characters are of different heights, one may look upwards and the other downwards (as we saw in Nelson Pimenta's *Frog and Ox* in Figure 11). Facial expressions associated with the different characters also help discriminate between them. Taking the example of tidying the room, in sign language, reference to the mother may use an exasperated but firm expression and reference to the child may use a grumpy and unwilling expression.

The embodiment of characters in signed storytelling is usefully mixed with classifiers to show changes in perspective in the action, similar to close-up and distant film shots, as we saw in the discussion of classifiers earlier. In Cristiane Esteves de Andrade's creative Libras piece *The Discovery*,[44] the central character is swept back in time to witness the start of the women's movement that led to International Women's Day on March 8 (see Figure 14). As she joins other women on a march, the central, embodied character is framed to the left and right by classifiers using the closed fists and forearms to represent the heads

---

[44] In Portuguese, *A Descoberta*. https://repositorio.ufsc.br/handle/123456789/200709.

(a)

(b)

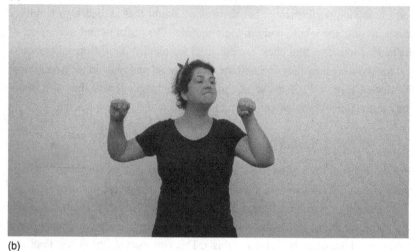

**Figure 14** Different perspectives shown through different classifier handshapes
in Cristiane Esteves de Andrade's *The Discovery*

**Source:** https://repositorio.ufsc.br/handle/123456789/200709.

and bodies of two other women.[45] This simultaneous use of embodiment and
classifiers that are close in size to the protagonist makes a powerful visual image
of solidarity. The perspective shifts to show the many women marching, using
open hand classifiers, with each finger representing a whole person. However,
the simultaneous use of the embodied character of the protagonist is also part of
the scene (as we can tell from the facial expression of anxious surprise), so we

---

[45] It also satisfying for Libras signers for whom the sign '8' also uses the closed fist, so the recurring
closed fist handshapes recall the date of International Women's Day.

(c)

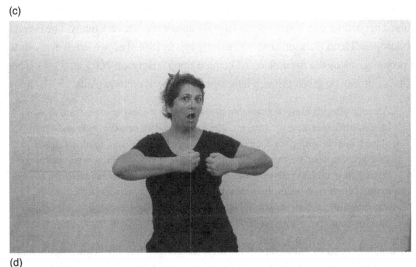

(d)

**Figure 14** (cont.)

see two perspectives at once. When the women link arms, we see this first through embodiment so that the hands and arms take the central embodied character's arms and then as a classifier sign in which the fully open hands are understood to represent many people moving forwards. In a conventional classifier sign, the fingers point upwards and are understood to represent an upright person (as in the second illustration in Figure 14), but in this novel classifier, they point downwards so that the linked thumbs become classifiers representing the linked arms of the women.

Although embodiment is commonly of human characters, it can be extended to non-humans. Animals and inanimate objects in sign language are given human characteristics through anthropomorphism. This portrayal of non-humans is highly valued in creative sign language, not least because it is often very funny. The French philosopher Henri Bergson observed as long ago as 1900 that 'we laugh every time a person gives us the impression of being a thing' (Bergson 2003, p. 33–4). This impression can be given through language, as he went on to explain:

> A comic effect is always obtainable by transposing the nature expression of an idea into another key. . . . Imagine ideas expressed in suitable style and thus placed in the setting of their natural environment. If you think of some arrangement whereby they are transferred to fresh surroundings, while maintaining their mutual relations, or, in other words, if you can induce them to express themselves in an altogether different style and to transpose themselves into another key, you will have language itself playing a comedy – language itself made comic. (Bergson 2003, p. 60)

Bergson was not thinking about sign language, but the same mechanism holds when creative signers take an image of something non-human and present that image in the 'new surroundings' of the human body. The audience perceives the transposition and laughs.

In her introduction to her poem *The Cat* (in *Bright Memory*, 1998, p. 26, but originally in *Gestures*, 1976), Dorothy Miles wrote: 'Using Ameslan [ASL], it's very easy to imitate animal characteristics and behaviour.' Arguably, 'it's very easy' because the language easily accommodates this imitation, but it takes considerable skill and wit for a signer to do it well. The skill lies in blending the human and animal characteristics, using both manual and non-manual elements.

We saw earlier in this section that embodying a person requires the signer to visualise clearly the appearance and behaviour of the human they wish to portray and map these onto their own appearance and behaviour using their own body. Embodying a non-human, however, requires some further stages. The signer must visualise the appearance and behaviour of the non-human and then map that from the non-human body onto the appearance and behaviour of a human body. Sometimes the body of the human signer has forms that map neatly onto the body of the non-human, either directly or by clear analogy. For example, the signer's head, eyes, and mouth can be used to represent the head, eyes, and mouth of an animal directly. Beyond this, the signer can choose body parts that are similar enough in form and location in relation to the rest of the body to represent the non-human. Thus, the arms can become branches and the fingers the twigs of a tree, where the human body stands for the trunk, or the outstretched arms can become the wings of a bird or an aeroplane. When referring to body parts that the human doesn't have as analogy, the hands can be used as 'body-part classifiers' to transfer the form of these onto the human. For example, we lack tails and antlers, but Gustavo Gusmão embodies animals with these in his creative piece *Deer vs Jaguar.*[46] He uses his human head, eyes, and body to represent those of the deer and his arms and hands are used by analogy to represent the deer's legs and hooves, and his hands also stand for the deer's antlers.[47] Later, his arms and hands represent the jaguar's legs, paws, and tail. In another piece *Aeroplane Flight,*[48] his arms become the aeroplane's wings and his face is the front of the fuselage. His hands, when located close to his upper chest, become the landing gear, in analogy with the location of the landing gear in relation to the wings. In this highly creative piece, the eyes and mouth also act as analogous parts for the runway landing lights, opening and closing rapidly as the lights flash.

Following Michiko Kaneko's division of anthropomorphic signing (see Sutton-Spence & Kaneko 2016), we may say that signers can show non-humans at the descriptive, pre-linguistic, and linguistic levels. At the descriptive level, animals and objects take human form merely because they are represented by the human body, but they are not attributed human thoughts, emotions, or desires. The deer, jaguar, aeroplane, and landing lights in Gustavo Gusmão's pieces have no human attributes apart from their form when he signs them. He achieves this effect particularly by keeping his facial expression to a minimum, avoiding the risk of betraying any human emotions on the face (see Figure 15).

At the pre-linguistic level of anthropomorphism, non-humans are portrayed with varying degrees of mental attributes usually associated with humans, showing emotions such as fear, bemusement, and pleasure. These are primarily communicated non-manually, often with exaggerated facial expression to create humour. Stefan Goldschmidt's *Golf ball*[49] is an entertaining example of anthropomorphism at the pre-linguistic level as the ball's emotions and desires are shown non-manually but the ball is not given the power of language to express itself fully. The head represents the ball (being analogous in shape) and the eyes and facial expression show how the ball feels as it takes part in the game of golf (see Figure 16). The signer's hands show the ground, cup, pin, tee, and club through classifiers, but these are never characters in the story and only the ball is embodied and anthropomorphised. Anthropomorphisation at this level is a popular form of creative signing because it is humorous (following Bergson's explanation of the human seen in non-humans).

At the linguistic level of anthropomorphism, non-humans are given the power to communicate by language. In creative signing, we see two different options for

---

[46] In Portuguese, *Veado vs onça.* https://youtu.be/r5vuNWZvytY.
[47] These are sometimes called body-part classifiers (see Johnston & Schembri 2007).
[48] In Portuguese, *Voo do Avião.* https://youtu.be/Io3e2eq1hOA.
[49] https://youtu.be/Gl3vqLeOyEE.

(a)

(b)

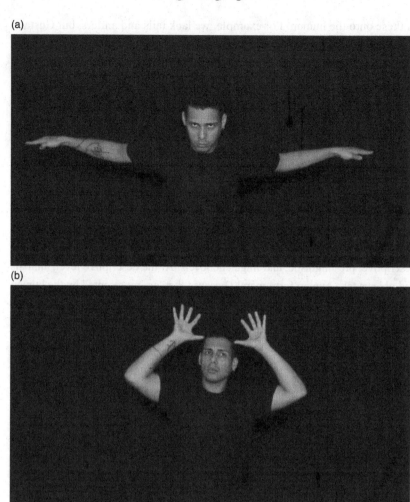

**Figure 15** Aeroplane and deer shown at the descriptive level of anthropomorphism in Gustavo Gusmão's *Aeroplane Flight* and *Deer vs Jaguar*
**Sources:** https://youtu.be/Io3e2eq1hOA and https://youtu.be/r5vuNWZvytY.

communicating linguistically. In the first option, the character may sign exactly like a human, even though we know it is not. This is seen in signed fables, as it is in spoken languages. For example, in the fable *The hare and the tortoise*, the two animals may be shown running in the way that hares and tortoises run, but when they converse, their signing is as though they were fully human. In the second option, the form of the animal may be carried over into their signing so that the hare signs with its paws and the tortoise with its broad front feet, and the relative length and mobility of their front limbs mean that the hare's signs are larger and

**Figure 16** Pre-linguistic level of anthropomorphism in Stefan Goldschmidt's
*Golf ball*
**Source:** https://youtu.be/Gl3vqLeOyEE.

less restricted, making use of the signer's arms, while the tortoise's signs are made
with the elbows tight into the sides and the hands against the signer's chest,
reflecting the shortness of the tortoise limbs. In these examples, part of the
entertainment lies in maintaining the handshape of the animal's limbs when
signing, distorting the signs, while still making them intelligible. For example,
a lion may sign with the hands always in the configuration of clawed paws, as in
Vanessa Lima's *Warrior Lioness*[50] where the sign 'tree' is made as though the
lion's paw signed it (see Figure 17).

*Filmic Productions – Multiple Perspectives*

Sign language literature is heavily influenced by film, another kinetic visual
storytelling art form. There are reports from many different countries of deaf
people enjoying retelling in sign language what they have seen in films, videos,
television programmes, or video games. All viewers learn the grammar of film
so that, for example, they can interpret images as different perspectives of the
same event or understand how images may be temporally or spatially organised
in film compared to the way that they are in reality. Much of this is reflected in
cinematic forms of creative signing that are sometimes termed *Visual
Vernacular* (or VV), a term coined by Bernard Bragg, who promoted and
developed a form of this filmic signing. It principally uses embodiment but
may also use classifiers of various types with the embodiment.

---

[50] In Portuguese, *Leoa Guerreira*. https://youtu.be/rfnKoCXmSg4.

**Figure 17** Sign created with the handshape determined by the animal's form in
Vanessa Lima's *Warrior Lioness*
**Source:** https://youtu.be/rfnKoCXmSg4.

This cinematic signing shows changes in perspective. The two perspectives
are usually seen sequentially so that we see first a person acting and then the
result of the action. Paul Scott's BSL poem *Tree*[51] embodies a man cutting a tree
with an axe and then embodies the tree as the axe cuts into it. Peter Cook's
highly visual work in ASL *Poetry*[52] repeatedly shifts back and forth between
two roles of an artist putting paint on a canvas and the canvas upon which the
paint is put. Anna Luiza Maciel's *Tinder*[53] embodies a woman swiping left and
right on her mobile phone and then shifts role to show the swiping from the
perspective of the phone (see Figure 18).

These multiple perspectives may also be shown simultaneously in what Paul
Dudis (2004) has termed 'body partitioning' and Christian Cuxac (2000) has
termed 'double transfer'. For example, the hands may be understood to belong
to one character and the face to another. In *Tinder*, when the phone reacts to the
swiping movements, the face and body portray the embodied phone, but the
hand is the embodied hand of the woman swiping. In Paul Scott's BSL poem
*Doll*,[54] in which a child puts make-up on an unwilling doll, we see two
characters and three perspectives simultaneously. In the first picture in
Figure 19, the artist has embodied the child, holding the doll firmly in his left
hand (we cannot see the doll, but we fill in the information in our imagination

---

[51] https://youtu.be/TaQIdovqsFg.
[52] In The Heart of the Hydrogen Jukebox at www.youtube.com/watch?v=aJ0Y-luT5_w.
[53] https://vimeo.com/267275098/a1289e263e.    [54] https://youtu.be/5iM7zbis68w.

(a)

(b)

**Figure 18** Two sequentially presented perspectives of a single action in Anna
Luiza Maciel's *Tinder*
**Source:** https://vimeo.com/267275098/a1289e263e.

because the context tells us this) and applying the doll's make-up with his right
hand. This is a single perspective of the scene. However, in the second picture in
Figure 19, the artist embodies two characters simultaneously and also shows
two simultaneous perspectives of the child. The face and body have taken the
role of the doll receiving the make-up on its eyes and objecting, but the hands
still embody the child's hands (not the doll's). The right hand applies the make-
up onto the embodied doll, not on the doll that is still held (invisible but
imagined) in the left hand.

(a)

(b)

**Figure 19** Two characters and three perspectives shown simultaneously in Paul
Scott's *Doll*

**Source:** https://youtu.be/5iM7zbis68w.

The perspectives may also be close-up and distant shots. We saw examples of
this in Cristiane Esteves de Andrade's piece *The Discovery* (see Figure 14). The
classifiers show the scene from a distance as we see the whole character moving
through space; the embodiment shows the scene in close-up, as we see only the
body of the character and none of the space surrounding the character. When
artists deliberately set out to create unfamiliar perspectives of familiar objects, we
see extra creativity at play. Ricardo Boaretto's piece entitled *Perspective*[55] shows

---

[55] In Portuguese, *Perspectiva*. https://repositorio.ufsc.br/handle/123456789/204191.

the heart of a sprinter as he runs. He embodies the sprinter to show his actions in a standard (although highly artistic) way but shows the beating heart through an unusual classifier in which the two hands in neutral space become the walls of the heart and move rhythmically to show it pumping hard (see Figure 20 (a)). He then shifts role to give a close-up image of the heart by embodying it completely, as his hands and arms show the walls of the heart (see Figure 20 (b)).

The embodiment seen in this filmic signing, VV, and other creative sign language genres is performance-led. It is in these highly visual creative pieces of filmic signing that the question of performance becomes especially important, but we need to consider it for all unwritten creative sign language. In many cases, separating the text from its performance may not be possible and may ultimately be minimally relevant to deaf audiences but focusing on performance elements of a piece helps us to understand and appreciate its richness.

## Beyond the Body – Mise-en-Scène, Special, and Visual Effects

Certain elements that are prepared before the performance include what is often termed mise-en-scène, such as background sets, costumes, and lighting. Although we might expect this principally in conventional theatre productions, these mise-en-scène performance elements are increasingly seen in other types of creative sign language performances.

What performers choose to wear and the background they stand against, whether for a live or recorded performance, can influence the impact of the piece. Ribeiro and Sutton-Spence (2021) note, for example, the difference between the clothes and background in performances of Ben Bahan's *Ball Story*[56] in ASL from 1989 and Sandro Pereira dos Santos' translation of it in Libras in 2009.[57] The contrast is striking between the formal button-down green shirt against a subtle, mostly grey, background in Ben Bahan's version and the loose white shirt worn with a necklace of large, coloured beads against a red background with an illustration of a golden ball emitting rays of light of Sandro Pereira's version. The Brazilian choice underpins a generally livelier and more playful performance, compared to the calm of the ASL version. Clothing can also deliver more subtle messages. In Bruno Ramos' Libras performance of the Brazilian national anthem,[58] the signer wears four different coloured shirts (blue, yellow, green, and white), reflecting the colours of the national flag. It is also performed variously against lush rainforest, within a traditional indigenous building or against a large stone wall symbolising the different heritages of the nation.

---

[56] https://www.facebook.com/watch/?v=1639328392762926.
[57] Available on the DVD *Piadas em Libras* and at https://youtu.be/kPXWu5UCTzk, with his kind permission
[58] https://youtu.be/STrLJipI18Q.

(a)

(b)

**Figure 20** Increasingly close-up perspectives of a beating heart in Ricardo Boaretto's *Perspective,* as a classifier and an embodiment

Source: https://repositorio.ufsc.br/handle/123456789/204191.

Backgrounds and costumes are often used in telling children's stories as part of the entertainment. In filmed stories, the signer's image can be superimposed upon a background of images from a storybook while the story is signed. The clothing of the storyteller is often deliberately selected to appeal to children by being informal and suggesting friendliness (in a way that wearing a black t-shirt against a blue background, conventional in other filmed genres, would be less attractive), but the storyteller can also dress as a character from the story. However, these costumes need to be chosen carefully to avoid confusion. For example, dressing in a red cape with a hood to tell the tale of Little Red Ridinghood may help the child identify with the principal character, but can create confusion when the performer embodies other characters such as the wolf and Grandmother.

Although there are examples of creative sign language on film from the first half of the twentieth century, filmed either by professional film crews or by amateur camera operators, there are relatively few (Supalla 1994). The rapid developments in creative sign language that began with the advent of widely accessible video recording after the 1980s have continued with increasingly sophisticated video editing programs.

One of the earliest examples we have of a signed poem is *The Death of Minnehaha,* performed by Mary Williamson Erd in 1913.[59] It is a translation of a written poem *Hiawatha*, written in English by Henry Longfellow. Her interpretation mixes dance, theatre, and aesthetic ASL. The piece is filmed outside, set among trees, and the performer is dressed in costume as Minnehaha. Any of these effects could have been achieved in a live performance but filming means over 100 years later, we still have access to the event. Krentz (2006) has described many of the implications of being able to record, preserve, and distribute works of sign language literature. His work focuses on availability of video and DVDs and was published in the same year as Google bought YouTube, beginning the era of easy sharing of videos on the internet.

Bartolomei and Pereira (2021) describe the elements that become relevant in creative sign language that has been recorded on video. Special effects may be added during filming, while the person is signing (Petry & Fischer 2014). This will include any interaction with props or other people and lighting, angle, and camera shot or even real effects such as smoke or running water. As well as these visual effects, Bartolomei and Pereira list shots, image treatment, speed, sound treatment, and graphic elements. Visual effects, however, are editing effects added after filming. They may include light filters or image speed and other images that are used either for illustration or with which the signer appears

---

[59] https://commons.wikimedia.org /wiki/File:Death_of_Minnehaha_(1913).webm.

to be interacting. These extra images can be stills, film, words, or numbers (e.g. dates) (Petry & Fischer 2014). Addition of images in children's stories is especially important to allow the children to link the pictures to the signs they see. It is less important but still enjoyable if done well in videos for older signers.

Films made using sign language enable signers to mix creative signing with these special and visual effects. The film *Violence* by Mãos em Fúrias[60] shows a text that is impossible to separate fully from its performance and film techniques. Some of the letters in this A-Z story rely on the film techniques, including different camera shots and angles, props, and other actors who don't sign but who nevertheless participate in the story and its structure. We will discuss this film in more depth in Section 3.

Multiple images of recordings of the same performance signed piece, or of different performances of the piece, can also be edited together in montage. Fernanda Machado's *Fallen Angel*[61] was filmed four times from different angles and with different distances of shot, and the four performances were then edited together to be seen at the same time. Because the timing of the signs was not identical in each performance, the signs are not synchronised in the montage version (Machado 2019). This technical manipulation of the poem was positively received by audiences (see Figure 21).

In this review of some of the principal visual devices used to create aesthetic effect in creative sign language we have referred to performances in a range of genres. The different origins, functions, and forms of creative sign language may lead to the use of different aesthetic devices. We will now address the question of the different genres, revealing the range of creative forms subsumed under the terms 'creative sign language' and 'sign language literature'.

## 3 Genres of Creative Sign Language

To understand the rich variety of creative sign language, it is useful to review the large number of diverse works and classify them. Without some sort of classification, we are faced with a number of examples that are hard to understand in any sort of systematic way. For members of the community who simply want to enjoy what they are seeing, this may not be especially important, but classification helps anyone who wants to understand the processes of creative signing, the products, and the way they are received by their audiences.

---

[60] In Portuguese, *Violência* by the group Mãos em Fúrias (Furious hands), starring Eduardo Tótoli, Luciano Canesso Dyniewicz, Elissane Zimmerman Dyniewicz and Carlos Alexandre Silvestri, directed by Giuliano Robert. https://youtu.be/8sYWSq2pwhg.
[61] In Portuguese *Anjo Caído*. https://vimeo.com/209842983.

**Figure 21** Montage of four recorded performances of Fernanda Machado's
*Fallen Angel*
**Source:** https://vimeo.com/209842983.

This classification is not straightforward, however. We saw at the beginning of Section 2 that ideas of translanguage help us to understand that sign languages are open systems and to appreciate the rich variety of visual resources available to sign language artists. Similarly, it is important to understand that national literatures are also not closed systems. As José Lambert (in Guerini et al. 2011, p. 29) observed: 'Both in terms of nation and in terms of language, literatures do not constitute homogeneous or closed communication systems, and interaction with other types of (literary) communication, of local or international origin, occurs at all times. . . . The cultural and linguistic complexity of every society implies the coexistence of various literary traditions in any sociocultural space.' Thus, we will proceed with our exploration of categories and genres while understanding that these categories are open and constantly interacting with each other.

In this section, we consider some examples of different categories of creative sign language that we classify generally as stories and poems. We may call these genres, understanding that there is no set way to determine genres and the hierarchies within them, so it is difficult to determine what are – or not – different genres at different levels of categorisation.

Since at least the time of Plato there have been attempts to classify different language art forms that we might wish to call literature. However, because literature is part of a dynamic and complex social system, how we classify creative works changes over time, as societies and their expectations of literature change. Elements cross over boundaries in a rich network of charac-teristics. We may wish, for example, to separate poems from stories, to under-stand better the characteristics of each. Or we may wish to separate adult literature from children's literature to highlight their different characteristics. We are then faced with four divisions of children's poetry, adult poetry, chil-dren's stories, and adults' stories. Perhaps we are interested in sign language literature from the twentieth and twenty-first centuries. This leads to a six-way division, involving poems or stories, each aimed at adults or children, and all of those from two different centuries. As we delve deeper, the networks become increasingly complex, leading us to accept that how we categorise and analyse our material depends on *why* we are attempting to classify the works.

It may appear helpful to take a 'top-down' approach and start with existing identified genres in written literature canons in languages such as English or Brazilian Portuguese and try to find examples of creative sign language that share characteristics with works in these genres. However, a bottom-up approach that looks at what deaf artists do and categorising their work according to its own characteristics may give us a clearer idea of what is valued within the deaf community. We should also remember that signers are familiar with the literary expectations of their surrounding hearing society so they may be influenced by a form or genre from the hearing world and develop it into a new signed genre.

For our purposes here, we classify genres of creative sign language according to elements related to their form, origin, author, target audience, subject matter, and function (Bahan 2006; Compagnon 1999). Within any of these categories, there will be questions of which sub-categories to include. We will proceed now, accepting that there is no simple, single, or correct way to determine genres but only ways that help us to understand and appreciate better what we see.

## Written Libras Literature

One important distinction in many studies of literature is whether the literature is written or essentially unwritten, with the characteristics of what is often called 'oral literature'. The written nature of most creative language called 'literature' in spoken languages has enabled a split between the text and its performance and a written text is understood to continue to exist even when it is not performed. Traditionally, commentaries on literature have assumed that it is written, and oral forms of literature are often (rightly or wrongly) considered to be a 'marked' or unusual form. In sign languages, however, most literature is unwritten, and the written form is marked.

In our review in Section 2 of some of the aesthetic ways in which creative sign language is foregrounded, we have seen that the 'text' and the 'performance' of creative pieces in sign languages are closely related. Indeed, it has been repeatedly claimed that sign language literature must be performed to exist because it is not written. However, recently we have come to recognise that it is possible to separate the performer from the text in sign languages when the artistic text is written, using a writing system such as SignWriting.

Few countries have deaf communities sufficiently familiar with SignWriting for artists and readers to produce and read written sign language literature, but Brazilian educators have made considerable effort over the last two decades to train students and teachers to read and write in Libras (Barreto & Barreto 2015). There is a growing number of examples of written Libras stories and poems (Barros 2020; Marquezi 2018). In these, the text is purely the text of the language piece, and each reader can apply their own performance to it.

Additionally, some poets have applied ideas of written concrete poetry to written Libras poems so that the written poem cannot be signed, any more than a concrete poem in a spoken language can be read aloud. Mauricio Barreto's *Swimming in the Pool*,[62] in Figure 22, lays out SignWriting ideograms on a page to create an image similar to a calligram[63] that tells a story which can be adapted into a signed version, but cannot be signed as it is presented.

Kacio Lima's written Libras poem *Community*, described in detail in Barros (2020), uses the written signs 'deaf', 'hearing', and 'signing', repeated and arranged on the page to produce the classic 'smiley face' icon. The individual written signs could be performed, but the visual effect of the written layout would be lost (see Figure 23).

Thus, written Libras poetry is an example of a genre of deaf literature, categorising it as distinct in some way from performed poetry.

## Humour

Humour is an element that runs through creative sign language poems, stories, theatre sketches, or jokes. We may say that humorous literature is defined by its function because its aim is to make us laugh. Traditionally, a lot of creative sign

---

[62] In Portuguese, *Nadar na piscina*.

[63] Calligrams are visual poems in written languages in which written words are arranged on the page in a form that relates to the meaning of the poem. The French poet Apollinaire created calligrams, such as *Reconnais-toi*, in which the words of the poem about a woman created the outline of a woman wearing a large-brimmed hat. Bourgeois (2020) shows examples of calligrams in French Sign Language.

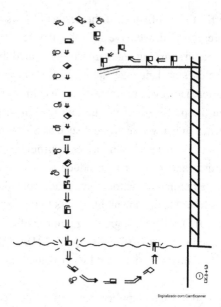

**Figure 22** Mauricio Barreto's *Swimming in the Pool* in SignWriting

**Source:** Barros 2020.

**Figure 23** Kácio Lima's *Community*

**Source:** Barros 2020.

language was performed to make people laugh, and this continues. We have seen that anthropomorphic signing, which has its roots in deaf folklore, is frequently very funny and can occur in a wide range of genres such as poetry, stories, or theatrical sketches and for different age groups. When thinking about humour and creative sign language, we can say that things may be funny because of their content (what we say) or their form (how we say it), although, of course, if the content and form are both funny, it's even funnier. The former, we may term deaf humour, with a focus more on the cultural elements of the humour. Deaf jokes or funny deaf stories, for example, may be retold in another language and the source of the humour is still clear. The latter we may call sign language humour, focusing on the language elements that produce it, and is lost when it is translated directly into another language. Susan Rutherford's (1989) reported joke that ends with the American deaf man writing 'Please BUT' in English to the hearing man at the railway level crossing is not remotely funny to anyone who does not know the ASL sign 'but'. The joke hinges on a pun: the ASL sign 'but' can also mean 'Open the barriers on a level crossing', which does not translate into English.

The most easily identifiable humorous genre in creative sign language is the joke, which may be defined as a short story with an unexpected ending, deliberately told with the expectation of making the audience laugh. Some jokes from wider hearing society are also told in the deaf community in sign language because the source of the humour is shared. However, in the genre of deaf jokes, the topics are of deaf people's world experiences and there is a deaf protagonist (Hessel 2015). Jokes have subgenres and many of them have a certain type of structure involving repetition, for example of actions or events. This may require two actions or events to occur in one way and the third to break the pattern of expectation that makes us laugh. In probably the best-known example of a traditional deaf joke, *Deaf Tree*, the lumberjack cuts a tree, shouts 'Timber!' and it falls. He cuts another tree, shouts 'Timber!' and it falls. He cuts a third tree, shouts 'Timber!' and it doesn't fall. Why? The tree was deaf. In *Deaf Lion*, a violinist plays his violin to send two hungry lions to sleep but before he can escape, a third lion approaches. It does not fall asleep when the violin plays and eats the violinist. Why? The lion was deaf.[64] There are also jokes that follow the three-way structure of 'a blind man, a man in a wheelchair and a deaf man', in which the first two characters behave in a way that conforms to expectations of their characters and then the deaf person behaves in

---

[64] There is another example, *Deaf Bull*, which is essentially the same joke but the characters are a Bullfighter, two hearing bulls that sleep when they hear the violin and the final deaf bull that does not sleep and tosses the bullfighter.

a different way – a way that is unexpected according to the structure of the joke, but is recognised expected deaf behaviour in the community, which makes it especially funny (Hessel, 2015; Hessel & Karnopp 2016; Sutton-Spence & Napoli 2012). In one joke of this type, God makes a blind man see and a man in a wheelchair walk, but the deaf man begs not to be made hearing because he doesn't want to lose his disability benefits. Thus, deaf jokes are fundamentally humorous because there is something in their content that makes us laugh.

Humour, however, can be created in different genres apart from jokes, both through content and the way it is signed. For example, humorous stories may have funny events throughout but are usually longer than jokes and do not necessarily have a punchline. Morgado (2011) lists five types of sign language humour, as ways to manipulate the language to make us laugh, irrespective of the content: imitations of films, people, animals, and objects presented through facial and body expressions; language games – often short stories – that play with handshapes, especially those used in the manual alphabet or number handshapes; games with movement; language games on taboo topics (in informal settings); jokes, cartoon drawings, and humorous anecdotes.

Hal Draper, a British deaf comedian, explained that sign language humour is strongly related to embodiment: 'it's about combining signing with facial expression, body movement, and with how Deaf people can become the thing. For hearing humour, I think the emphasis is based on the English words, but for Deaf people it is related to role shift, facial expression, and things like that' (Interview conducted by Jenny Smith in 2005 and cited in Boldo & Sutton-Spence 2020). The facial expression and body movement in the embodiment are frequently exaggerated to create stronger comic effect.

Sign language humour is also created by manipulating the form of signs in what Klima and Bellugi (1979) called 'Wit and Plays on signs' (p. 319), where different meanings are blended through similar sign forms. Signers may 'substitute one regular ASL prime value for another. . . . This occurs when a signer intentionally distorts a sign by substituting a value that adds a new dimension of meaning' (1979, p. 324). In this, any of the principal parameters of signs (handshape, location, movement, orientation, and number of hands) can be substituted for another. For example, the Libras sign meaning 'interesting' is made with a curved index finger bending and moving forward from the eye. When a signer was asked if he found something interesting (using the conventional sign), he replied that he found it 'very interesting', using all four fingers instead of the index finger. Articulating one sign on each hand allows signers play with sign antonyms (e.g. simultaneously signing 'smiling' and 'frowning', 'confident' and 'shy', or 'want' and 'don't want', one on each hand). The incongruity of seeing the two signs at the same time can be funny. In blending, the signer alters the parameter of two (or more) signs to link their form and meaning in a way that creates a new, humorous meaning.

Humorous signing is almost by definition creative because novelty, seeing new takes on familiar ideas, is the source of the humour. Once the form has become established and familiar, it is no longer amusing. In Brazil, when a person sneezes, one may say to them 'health!' ('saúde!' in Portuguese), equivalent to the English 'bless you!'. The conventional location of the sign 'health' in Libras is on the chest. The first time someone signed 'health!' in Libras at the nose rather than on the chest, it was a witty blend of the location of the sign 'nose' with the movement and handshape of the sign 'health'. Now it is simply what one signs when someone sneezes. People may still smile at the entertaining sign, but the novelty is gone.

Acknowledging that humour can occur in almost any genre, we will now turn to the two traditional main genres in literature of prose (in the form of stories) and poetry. Our discussion is not exhaustive but aims to show some of the rich diversity of creative sign language.

## Stories

### Narratives of Personal Experience

These stories are a core genre of deaf literature, categorised primarily by their origin because they are stories that deaf people tell about their experiences as a deaf person (things that would not happen to a hearing person). These narratives of personal experience are often as important for the teller to tell as for the audience to learn about other people's experience. When they are shared, people can feel a closer bond as members of the same community, especially deaf children who see deaf adults tell stories of how things were when they were young. Some deaf people are known within their community as good story-tellers who have interesting stories to tell but is important for everyone's sense of identity to be able to share stories of their own experience. When we talk about creative sign language, we often talk about canonical stories, jokes, or poems, as specific instances of a genre, but narratives of personal experience are too varied for us to select any as 'examples'.

### Filmic Monologues of Visual Vernacular

We discussed some aspects of filmic VV monologues in the section 'Filmic Productions – Multiple Perspectives' when we considered multiple perspectives in filmic performances. The genre of VV has its origins in mime, and especially in films made by non-deaf people. Not only is the film's plot reproduced but so is the visual form of the film. In a film, people act against a backdrop of scenery, shown from different camera angles and in shots of different length and distance. If there is a part of the film where people are seen in close-up and distance shots, the signed filmic monologues telling the story of the film use signed techniques of classifiers and embodiment to show this (and does not use the conventional vocabulary of any specific named sign language). If a piece of the film is in slow motion, the signs can also be in slow motion; if it cuts rapidly between shots, the signer shows this by cutting rapidly from one sign to the next. If the film rewinds so we see events as though time is running backwards, the signer signs backwards (Bauman 2003, 2006; Monteiro 2023).

It has long been common for a person to sign from memory the film that they saw, but technology now makes it possible for a person to film themselves signing what is shown in the film while showing the original film in a separate section of the screen.

Although filmic signing is historically based on real films, the techniques may also be used as a storytelling technique for original deaf stories. The story may be fictional or perhaps a historical event, but they are portrayed using those same techniques. Filmic monologues can also be seen in poems and even those as short as haiku.

Visual vernacular is popular worldwide because of its accessibility to signers from different countries and there are so many examples available that it is impossible to name all the artists who produce and circulate this genre of work. From the older works of artists such as Bernard Bragg, Guiseppe Giuranna, Guy Bouchauveau, Peter Cook, and Richard Carter, we can only mention few names of younger talented performers of the genre worldwide, such as Ace Mahbaz, Cristiano Monteiro, Dack Virnig, Edyta Kozub, Erwan Cifra, Justin Perez, Modiegi Njeyiyana, Nicola Della Maggiora, and Renata Freitas. They, and many others whom we cannot mention here, are all developing and promoting the art form on various internet platforms, and we strongly encourage readers to explore it further. For research published in English on VV and filmic monologues we recommend van Brandwijk (2018) and Asmal and Kaneko (2020).

### Original Constraint Stories

Ben Bahan (2006) describes some examples of signed literature that follow constraints. For example, the piece may use a single handshape, alternate between two handshapes, or follow a set series of handshapes such as those of numbers or the letters of the manual alphabet.

Number constraint stories must use signs with handshapes that follow the order of numeral signs, usually starting from zero or one and going to nine or ten. They can go in reverse, from ten to zero, or from zero to ten and back to zero again. In Cristiane Esteves de Andrade's complex performance piece *Zero vs Nine*,[65] the number handshapes in signs on the left hand go from nine to zero, while the numbers on the right hand go from zero to nine. This is a remarkable physical feat, as well as creative one. Number stories are also popular in children's stories and language games. Juliana Lohn's *The Animals (numbers)*[66] and *Crazy Bird (numbers)*[67] are two examples.

In bilingual signed constraint pieces, signs use the handshapes of letters of the manual alphabet as they spell out words in the written language. The topic usually has something in common with the word they spell out. For example, Anna Luiza Maciel's short story *Sol* (in English 'Sun') uses signs with handshapes that are the same as the letters S, O, and L to describe someone creeping out early on a sunny morning.[68] This story is aimed at young children, and ABC constraint stories have widespread application in didactic children's literature. Importantly, the signs, when translated into the language in which the signer reads don't need to start with the same letter. The signs 'asleep', 'sunrise', and 'sunshine' in Libras are made with the handshape that is the same as the manual letters S, O, and L, but have no connections with the initial letters of their Portuguese translations 'adormecida', 'nascer do sol', and 'luz do sol' (see Figure 24).

The A-Z story is one type of constraint story in which the signer attempts to tell a story using signs that use the handshape of individual manual letters in the order in which they occur in the whole alphabet. A-Z stories were brought to Brazil in 1999 by Nelson Pimenta, who had studied in the USA and learned ABC stories in ASL. His *The Painter A-Z* remains a Libras classic, and A-Z and other letter-related constraint stories are now widespread, especially when they are used as teaching tools. However, A-Z stories are not merely for children (Rutherford 1993 observed that they were often told by adolescents in the USA) and in another example of crossing genres, ABC stories can move out to film.

The Brazilian short film *Violence*[69] is an A-Z story that tells of a dream of violent revenge. The film uses linguistic, performance, and technical effects to tell the story and to show the different letters. For the letter A the actor presses the call button of the lift (see Figure 25 (a)). If simply signing, this action would be shown with the same movement and handshape, but in the real-world context, the man does press the call button, thus the sign and the action on the

---

[65] In Portuguese *Zero vs Nove*, https://repositorio.ufsc.br/handle/123456789/209171.
[66] In Portuguese *Os Animais (números)* https://vimeo.com/showcase/6241328/video/348189766.
[67] In Portuguese *Pássaro (números)* https://vimeo.com/showcase/6241328/video/348080802.
[68] https://vimeo.com/showcase/6241328/video/444383947.
[69] Mentioned in section 2. Available at https://youtu.be/8sYWSq2pwhg.

(a)

(b)

(c)

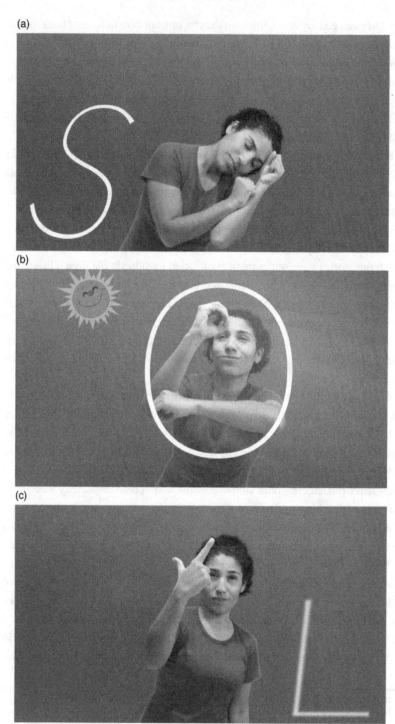

**Figure 24** *Sun* (Sol) by Anna Luiza Maciel
**Source:** https://vimeo.com/showcase/6241328/video/444383947.

object in the real world complement each other. For B, the lift doors open. We see the lift doors opening and the sign for lift doors opening, so the same information is presented in two different ways. In C, the character pulls a chair back, using the C handshape of a handling classifier. This sign's meaning would be unclear without the visual context of the real chair, but without the actor using this handshape, the chair would not move, so the sign and the object each contributes to the meaning of the event. The letter Ç uses the same handshape as C but with a shaking movement. In the film, the character holds a box using this handshape and shakes it. The Libras signs 'deaf' and 'make-a-mistake' use the G and H handshapes, respectively, but they do not use props or images from the film to add any meaning and so stand alone as signs. For the L handshape, the protagonist takes a gun from a box. The box is a real prop; the gun is only signed (see Figure 25 (b)). For M, the conventional classifier to show three people advancing in a line is inverted. Instead of the fingertips pointing upwards, they point downwards. This classifier handshape is reinforced by a carefully framed image of the legs of the three actors advancing (see Figure 25 (c) and (d)). The letter O is shown from an unusual perspective, focusing on the space between the fingers, rather than the fingers, to show the barrel of the imagined gun (see Figure 25 (e)). The letters W, X, and Y are not spelled out by manual letters at all but instead are formed by people lying on the ground after the act of dream violence. The camera focuses on only the legs of three actors in the W formation, the forearms of two people are lying across each other, in an X shape and one more lies with his arms above his head, making a Y shape.

## Children's Literature

Children's literature is an example of a genre determined principally by its intended audience. Although, like all literature, its function is to entertain, it usually has an underlying didactic function. There are many examples of signed translations of children's books and of retellings of traditional children's stories (some of them inspired by films and cartoons), fables, and folktales. There are also increasing numbers of original deaf creative signed stories and poems aimed at children. These have the advantage that they can be constructed from the basis of deaf culture and the underlying structure of sign languages.

Nursery rhymes and language games for the very young are a genre that forms a crucial part of the shared childhood experience of children in any community. Short songs and poems that are highly repetitive and have strong rhythms and clear rhymes encourage children to focus on forms in their language. This is just as true in sign languages as in spoken languages. Andrews and Baker (2019, p. 5) observe that ' Nursery rhymes in American

**Figure 25** Signs, props, and visual effects in the A-Z film *Violence* (*Violência*) by Mãos em fúrias, showing the letters A, L, M, and O

**Source:** https://youtu.be/8sYWSq2pwhg.

(d)

(e)

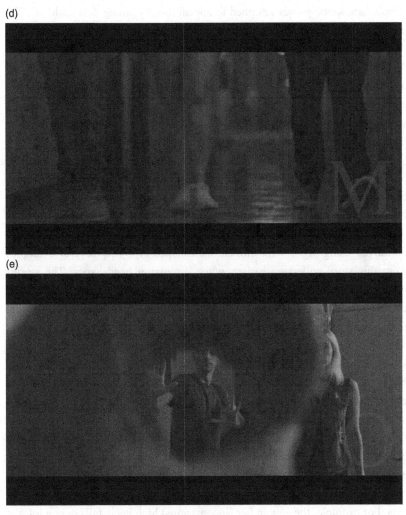

**Figure 25** (cont.)

Sign Language (ASL) can be used ... to support early acquisition of sign language, ASL literacy, and emergent English literacy. As a form of children's ASL literature, ASL nursery rhymes manipulate the abstract, sub lexical, or phonological structure of signs to provide children with playful language experiences.'

Although short poems and language games are used with young deaf children (Blondel and Miller 2001 describe nursery rhymes in French Sign Language), there is not a widespread tradition of nursery rhymes in sign languages, possibly because most deaf children are born to hearing parents, so are rarely exposed to the sign language of native signers before the age of five. However, there are simple handshape games designed to appeal to very young deaf children. The deaf duo Hands Land, for example, has created short rhythmic signed songs in ASL for deaf children aged zero to six, with brightly coloured illustrations.[70] The idea is to use repetition of different signed parameters, such as handshape or location, or repeating collocations of two signs of different grammatical classes such as nouns and adjectives or nouns and verbs to help children learn and play with signs. Crucially, the aim is to encourage children to think about and explore their language creatively, using basic principles of sign formation.

Signed stories aimed at very young children should be short (about one minute), visually attractive, and preferably funny. They also need large, brightly coloured illustrations to maintain the child's attention and to help them link the information in the pictures to the signs presented. In Brazil, the stories created for the 'Didactic Literature in Libras' showcase[71] are short Libras narratives using signs with similar handshapes. We saw several examples from this story collection earlier, when discussing handshapes. The stories were composed and performed by skilled, experienced deaf storytellers who could act as sign language models for the children. They are highly visual, following the devices and norms of signed literature that we outlined in Section 2 and deliberately highlight sign language structure, using carefully selected handshapes and placement of signs, gaze direction, facial expression, body movement, and the rhythm and timing of the signs. Exaggeration is especially funny for children, so the stories use exaggerated facial expressions and sign movements.

The stories have a single character, which is linguistically easier for young children, and the character is a deaf animal because young children enjoy anthropomorphic stories. Children in this age group find incongruity, slapstick, and bodies funny (Luckner & Yarger 1997), so the stories include these elements. For example, the cow in her (incongruous) high heels falls over a lot, the monkey is smelly, and the ant is shocked to find she is naked.

One genre of signed literature currently underserved is that for deaf adolescents and young adults. Many deaf children grow up without access to sign language and only encounter it in their teens. There is little sign language literature for this target audience and few original deaf stories told for these more mature language beginners and yet it should be the ideal way to encourage them to engage in learning sign language and its literature (Spooner 2016). This is an area that needs more development to catch up with the widespread availability of Young Adult literature for hearing teenagers.

---

[70] See, for example, their introductory video at https://youtu.be/zKrpkBY23eg.
[71] In Portuguese, 'Literatura didática em Libras', https://vimeo.com/showcase/6241328.

We will leave our discussion of original deaf-authored stories here but will return to another type of creative sign language story when we consider translated pieces in a further section.

## Poems

Sign language poetry may be defined as the highest form of original signed performance art of deaf communities. The aesthetic language is carefully polished and chosen to maximise emotional impact through clear, powerful visual images. The language is strongly foregrounded, so that form is usually more important than content. Indeed, audiences often need to think carefully about the form of language to find the meaning, which may be obscure on first viewing. Sign language poems also tend to be short (Machado 2017) and rhythmic. Signed poetry in the 1980s and 1990s often used obtrusively regular repetition of sub-sign parameters, especially handshape, to create an effect analogous to rhyme and alliteration, and this attention to language form continues, although the emphasis on creating visual images has become as important, if not more so, in some forms of sign language poetry.

The genre of poetry is a relative newcomer in creative sign language. There is a sociocultural impact from calling something 'poetry' because the term accords it a status above that of other creative forms. For many years, although some deaf communities had an art tradition of translating written poems into sign languages, as Ormsby observes, 'No poetic register existed in ASL because poetic expression in sign was socially inconceivable and as long as it remained socially inconceivable it was linguistically pre-empted' (1995, p. 113). Now, however, the social status of sign languages has made the idea of poetry acceptable.[72]

Ormsby's research, published in 1995, found that 'No set of traditional poetic formulae is passed along from generation to generation . . . Thus far, the devices that structure ASL verse . . . are by and large individual rather than conventional' (1995, p. 169). However, poetic conventions have developed since that time. Bearing in mind that it is not easy even to identify and define a text as a poem and harder still to identify genres in sign language poetry, we will now outline some conventionalised poetic genres that are emerging, considering haiku, performance challenge poems, duets, classifier and garden path poems, theme-driven poems such as deaf-related and horror, and Slam poetry.

---

[72] And, conversely, poetry can confirm the status of the language, with the reasoning that a language that has a poetry must be a language with status.

## Haiku

Haiku is a genre that has crossed over from written poetry into sign language poetry to become its own established genre in sign languages. Kaneko (2008) lists the five essential features of traditional Japanese haiku poems as brevity, implicitness, simplicity, objectivity, and concreteness. The primary aim of haiku is to produce the greatest possible meaning in the fewest words. Kaneko quotes the English haiku poet Alan Summers, saying that they are 'six-second poems' (Kaneko 2008, p. 52). Traditionally, haiku is made of seventeen sounds or syllables, divided into three lines of five, seven, and five, but its 'concise form and rich imagery has attracted many people outside Japan, including Deaf people in the western world' (Kaneko 2008, p. 8), so the traditional poetic form has changed as the haiku form has been adopted into other languages. For example, the conventions of seventeen syllables divided between three lines have mostly been discarded in sign language haiku. Haiku poems are rarely metaphorical and do not overtly refer to abstract and imaginary things, but rather present images that can be directly perceived by the senses, especially vision. Although any of the five key features of haiku poems do occur in sign languages, Kaneko considers that only brevity is consistently maintained.

Japanese haiku translated into English encouraged English-writing poets to produce their own original work. ASL artists created their own translations of English-language haiku using poetic principles of highly visual signing, and so established the genre in sign language.[73] Deaf artists such as Dorothy Miles and Robert Panara promoted sign language haiku in the USA. The genre spread from the USA to many countries, including the United Kingdom via Dorothy Miles and was revitalised by Michiko Kaneko's research in the early years of this century. Haiku came to Brazil from the United Kingdom and Sweden (brought by deaf poets influenced by Kaneko's work), where it has become established and is now taught as a way to encourage succinct, strong visual poetic signing.

Kaneko (2008) has argued that haiku poems in sign language are the result of 'fusion of two different poetic traditions: the lineage of traditional Japanese art form and the rich heritage of Deaf art and poetry'. Both forms are noticeably short, highly condensed, economical forms of poetry, and the themes and content are often shared when the poems describe images from nature. However, Japanese haiku poems are minimalist, and the language is 'objective, detached, and non emotional' (2008, p. 9), while the language in signed haiku is often 'highly expressive and emotional'. Additionally, haiku poems by deaf

---

[73] A recording of Robert Panara's translations filmed in 1984 is available at https://youtu.be /faJfH8yUECU (starting at 12:52).

signers may touch on issues explicitly related to deaf people's experiences. Signed haiku poems often have three clear parts (roughly, a beginning, a development, and an end) and may only use three signs – one for each part. They may follow the norms of other signed poetry, such as deliberate selection and use of handshape, rhythmic signing, and non-manual components.

João Raphael Bertoncelli's *Calling the Cattle* (mentioned in Section 2) is a good example of Libras haiku. As well as being short, simple, and emotionally neutral, with carefully chosen signs, it is on the topic of nature, a common characteristic in haiku. Nigel Howard's *Deaf*[74] is a signed haiku with a deaf-related theme. The first five rhythmical signs of the poem share the same flat hand 'B' handshape, describing the birth of a deaf child and the parents' trust in the medical profession. The final, sixth sign, changes rhythm and handshape as the baby has cochlear implants imposed upon it. The poem is short, the language is simple, and even the final shocking sign of implantation is delivered with neutral emotion, but it can stimulate a powerful reaction in audiences.

## Performance Challenge Poems

All signed poems require an element of skilled performance, but performance challenge poems focus on technical issues and the physical challenges of movement. Examples in traditional deaf folklore are fingerspelling different words on opposing hands. Mary Beth Miller's *Live at SMI!* tells the story of learning to simultaneously spell CAT on one hand and COW on the other. This is not at all easy for humans whose bodies and brains appear wired for the two hands to mirror each other – mirroring is common in deaf children learning to sign (Pichler et al. 2019) and most two-handed signs are symmetrical. Battison's (1978) symmetry constraint in the phonetic-phonological theory of sign languages is ultimately premised on human physiology that precludes non-symmetrical movements. There is a reason why patting your head and rubbing your stomach is a party trick – it is contrary to how we are wired. Breaking the symmetry link is satisfying to watch. It is not simply a matter of holding one handshape while making a different one on the other hand, but the handshapes must change to be different from the previous ones and different from each other at the same time. Cristiane Esteves de Andrade's poem *Zero vs Nine* is an excellent example of numbers going in two directions on opposite hands, with the added pleasure that the numbers are a delimited story so that the handshape is also a sign and not only a number. Fernanda Machado's *V & V*[75] involves the V handshape on each hand at different orientations that moves in different directions that are not symmetrical. These performance challenge poems are

---

[74] https://www.youtube.com/watch?v=xitL4etCCgI.    [75] https://vimeo.com/325444221.

not mere party tricks, however, but also use poetic devices and form. They need to have content, whether the content is abstract or tells a story.

## Duets

Another performance-related genre is that of duet signed poems in which two performers act jointly to co-create the piece, blending language and performance elements. Although we focus on duets in Libras and ASL, here, we note that poetic duets are common in deaf communities in many countries, for example *Grazie* (2001) by Rosaria and Giuseppe Giuranna in Italy,[76] *Fashion Times*[77] and *Deaf Gay*[78] (both 2011) by Paul Scott, Richard Carter, and David Ellington in the United Kingdom and *Unexpected Moment*[79] (2014) by Jamila and Amina Ouahid in Sweden.

Signed duets offer several different spatial and language options. The signers can position themselves side by side, front and back, or above and below. In any of these cases, they can change their relative positions during the duet. In a front-and-back duet, the person standing behind can emerge, so that the two signers stand side by side. In side-by-side duets, the signers can move closer or further away from each other and turn to face each other or face forwards.[80]

A good example of a front-back duet is 'four arms language' in *Poetry* by the Flying Words Project, from which the illustration at the beginning of this Element is taken.[81] As they sign 'I can play with language', they literally play with the sign 'language', as they make a four-handed sign 'language' that moves in all directions with the hands of the rear signer contacting the hands of the front signer, producing enjoyably symmetrical, rhythmic movements.

Anna Luiza Maciel and Sara Amorim's poem *Libras Law*[82] is a side-by-side duet. In this poem, some signs are articulated individually and some jointly. In Figure 26, the performers independently sign the two-handed sign 'law' and then create it together, using one hand each.

Coordinating the signing of the two artists is satisfying because of the skill required and the wit when they create signs that could not be possible without a second person. Pedroni (2021) has shown that it is possible for one person to sign what is produced in a duet, for example, by producing the signs in sequence

---

[76] *Grazie* (in English, *Thanks*) www.youtube.com/watch?v=xFohb9nBKig.
[77] https://youtu.be/DFKASTB-LHw.      [78] https://youtu.be/3DS5xGW8jcQ.
[79] https://youtu.be/hD48RQLQurg.
[80] In *Psychotic Memory* by Debbie Rennie and Peter Cook the signers start with their backs to the audience.
[81] There are several recordings of this poem available, including at https://youtu.be/8nMqYym4Mws.
[82] In Portuguese, *Lei de Libras*. https://vimeo.com/267274663/87da6783f2.

(a)

(b)

**Figure 26** Side-by-side duet *Libras Law* by Anna Luiza Maciel and Sara
Amorim signed separately and jointly
**Source:** https://vimeo.com/267274663/87da6783f2.

rather than simultaneously or by the audience imagining the missing signs but
that the visual aesthetics suffer.

### Deaf-Related

Deaf-related theme poems is the first of two genres based on form and content
that we will describe here.

There was a period in the twentieth century when the topic of 'deaf poetry'
needed to be deafness. Genres change and now a 'deaf poem' can be on any

topic, if it is composed by a deaf person, aimed primarily at deaf people, on a subject that appeals to deaf people and presented in a way to appeals to deaf audiences. However, a subgenre of poems on a topic of deafness, *Five Senses*, sits squarely within deaf literature. The original poem that gave rise to the genre is the BSL poem *Five Senses* by Paul Scott.[83] It follows the advice given to many creative writers to describe the world in their writing using the experience of all five senses – what is seen and heard and what can be known through touch, taste, and smell. Paul Scott's original poem shows how sight and hearing work together for a deaf person, through creative use of handshapes, finishing with a simple, novel handshape (not used in conventional BSL) that says simply 'this is me'. The poem was translated into Libras by Nelson Pimenta[84] and since then other poets have attempted to create poems and vignettes to describe the deaf world experience in a positive way, without signing 'deaf' but alluding to all the senses. *Five Senses* poems are deaf creative pieces that describe the world through a deaf person's experience. The challenge to the artist is to show how hearing is replaced by different senses so the deaf person lacks nothing.

### Horror

In *The Heart of the Hydrogen Jukebox*, Peter Cook describes how students at NTID experimented with signing the monsters they saw in Heavy Metal comic books. Signing other worldly creatures was already part of deaf creativity – the deaf poet Eric Malzkuhn described his ASL translation of Lewis Carrol's *Jabberwock* poem as the first break with staid translated poems, in which he signed fantastical creations based on the illustrations of the poem. The visual creation of monsters has led to the new genre of 'horror poems', drawing on horror films and films about the supernatural, including attacks by aliens, zombies, and ghosts. As far as we know, this genre has not yet been described in other sign languages, but it is well-established in Libras. Suspense is built through timing, changes in perspective, and embodiment, but the defining characteristic of this genre is the way the monsters are presented using novel classifiers and embodiment.

### Classifier and Garden Path Poems

Classifier poems do not use conventional signs but require the artist to use only classifier handshapes that present and describe referents, rather than naming them. The pleasure for audiences lies in the strong visual images presented and in the satisfaction of identifying the referents without their being named.

---

[83] https://youtu.be/-qLcuxfdoYY.
[84] As *Cinco Sentidos*, available at https://youtu.be/AyDUTifxCzg.

Paul Scott's poem *Tree*[85] is an example of a classifier poem, in which all the characters and their actions are shown using whole entity or handling classifiers. Although Paul Scott is a BSL poet, the classifier poem is internationally intelligible. The poem has given rise to an entire subgenre of Libras poetry, in which signers use classifiers to present a tree and create a poetic narrative around it.

In Paul Scott's *Tree*, once the entity classifier for the tree has been placed in signing space, the hand signing the tree is removed and shows other referents moving relative to or interacting with the tree. Even though the tree is not signed again, signers know that it is understood to be there and when a ladder is leaned in apparently empty space, we know it is leaning against the tree. When the blind person's cane taps an empty space at that location, we understand that the cane is tapping against the tree. In this classifier poem, viewers simply enjoy the map of visual images that are built up.[86]

However, classifiers and the understanding of these 'empty spaces' can also create Garden Path poems,[87] poems that fool the audience into expecting one thing, when it is another. Poets and authors often mislead readers for the sake of the impact of a piece, for example, leading the reader to assume a character is male rather than female or vice versa. As classifiers are underspecified for their meaning, they are the foundation of this genre in sign languages. Robert Fonseca's poem *Fooled*[88] uses an entity classifier, as it shows a person hastily packing, clearly late for a flight. The classifier handshape used for an aeroplane shakes to show the aeroplane getting ready for take-off until the person reaches out to grab it and talks into it. Then we understand that it is the vibration of a mobile phone ringing, and not the plane taking off. The trip down the garden path occurs because the entity classifier handshape to refer to an aeroplane and a phone are the same.

Handling classifiers are also used for garden path poems, where the context misleads viewers about what is being handled or how it is handled, relying on the expectation of viewers seeing what is not there. Johanna Mesch's *Party*[89] seems to portray a suicide when a jilted woman holding a knife appears to stab herself and audiences are surprised (and relieved) when the woman sits up again, apparently alive and well. The twist occurs because the sign used for the stabbing is a handling classifier, so we only see the hand holding the knife handle and need to imagine the blade. The context fools us into assuming that

---

[85] https://youtu.be/TaQIdovqsFg.

[86] *Tree* is an excellent teaching resource for language and literature because it encourages use of rhythm and creative new classifiers. Beginners can use classifier handshapes that already exist. More advanced signers and skilled creative signers can use new classifier handshapes.

[87] So called because they lead the viewer 'down the garden path', misleading or deceiving them.

[88] In Portuguese *Enganado*, https://repositorio.ufsc.br/handle/123456789/204138.

[89] https://youtu.be/s8BLY1Nm7qQ.

the blade is pointing towards the woman, but careful observation of the orientation of the handshape in the performance shows that the blade is pointing *away* from the chest when the handle hits it.

## Slams

Poetry slams are a relatively new genre of poetry, defined by their function and context, growing out of an oral tradition of verbal duels in spoken languages. Slams, when held as a contest, have rules that the participants must follow. The poems are time-limited (usually three minutes, which is also the upper limit that is usually considered comfortable for creative sign language pieces, especially poems) and props, music, or anything external to the poem that adds to its meaning beyond the performance are not permitted. Importantly, the poem must have been composed by the performer. The thoughts and feelings expressed by the poet can be highly personal and are frequently sociopolitical, demanding political change and social justice. Many of these rules have crossed into sign language poetry slams. ASL poetry slams have been run in the USA since 2005 and have been especially associated with New York and the guidance of Douglas Ridloff, but sign language slams now occur worldwide. In Brazil, some slams are deaf-only (or at least Libras only), but slams are also an opportunity for deaf poets and creative sign language artists to interact with hearing spoken word artists. Deaf and hearing people team up to produce their own duet forms that go beyond a simple voiced interpretation of the signed poem to blend the signing and voicing to create additional meaning. The hearing member of the team may sign with the deaf artist and the deaf artist may speak. Not all slams are competitive, and many are simply opportunities for new artists to share their sign language work informally in front of a supportive audience. Importantly, though, Libras slams offer a forum for social politics to be expressed in the deaf community. The politics can concern the place of deaf people in society, highlighting audism and the social and linguistic oppression of deaf people demanding equal respect and rights for the deaf community. Slam poems can also be of other politics, addressing gender, race, and LGBT+ inequalities (Júnior & Pereira 2020; Santos, Grigolom, & Medeiros 2020).

Although this review has been necessarily selective, it shows the growing range of genres in sign language poetry.

## *Translations and Adaptations*

Most of the creative sign language that we have showcased in our discussions is original work by deaf artists with its origin in the deaf community. However, we must also briefly address issues of translated sign language literature. Stephen

Ryan in 1993 outlined three kinds of ASL storytelling: original, adaptation, and translation, and these can be extended to other creative sign language genres such as poems and jokes.

In some senses, any translation of a literary work is also an adaptation, as it should seek to create similar effects in the source language and target language readers. However, in creative sign language, the idea of adaptation often refers specifically to adding references to deaf people and their experiences in a story. For example, non-deaf classic or traditional children's stories and fables may be adapted so that perhaps the three little pigs, Red Riding Hood, or Cinderella are deaf and behave in culturally approved 'deaf ways'.

Adaptation also occurs when creative sign language works are translated between sign languages of different national cultures. Nelson Pimenta's Libras translation of Ben Bahan's ASL story *Bird of a Different Feather* includes a scene with an Afro-Brazilian healer, adapted from the original scene of a North American Native American healer. In Paul Scott's original poem *Tree*, the human passer-by is a blind man, and the animals are a dog and a cat. Brazilian adaptations make the human a Saci (a folkloric sprite), and the animals a spotted jaguar and a parrot, or from north-eastern Brazil, a cowboy, a horse, and an exhausted, thirsty cow in a drought.

Although there are examples of translations between sign languages, as in these examples, they are relatively rare. This may be partly because the shared visual-spatial grammars of sign languages make the source sign language easier to understand than in most spoken languages, especially in works that rely less on conventionalised signs and more on highly iconic structures. However, it may also be because deaf poet-translators have not yet engaged much with the task. Nelson Pimenta's Libras translation of Paul Scott's BSL *Five Senses*[90] and Sandro Pereira dos Santos' Libras translation[91] of Ben Bahan's ASL *Ball Story*[92] show the potential for such translations (Ribeiro & Sutton-Spence 2021).

The bulk of translated literature in sign languages currently is in the field of children's literature. There are many examples of children's stories told in sign language by storytellers and translators (deaf and hearing). As it is children's literature, there is a direct or underlying didactic purpose behind the translations, and the aim is often to encourage and develop spoken language literacy skills in deaf children and encourage bilingualism in their signed and written languages. While it is important for deaf children to see good-quality storytelling in sign language, the translators should adapt the works to the literary norms

---

[90] As *Cinco Sentidos*, https://youtu.be/AyDUTifxCzg.
[91] Available on the DVD *Piadas em Libras* and at https://youtu.be/kPXWu5UCTzk, with his kind permission.
[92] https://www.facebook.com/watch/?v=1639328392762926.

of their deaf community. Most translation policies tacitly assume that the source language of the primary text should be the written one, but it should be equally as possible to translate original signed texts into the written language, privileging deaf perspectives (Schlemper 2021). Unfortunately, translations from signed texts to written or spoken ones are far less common than those in the other direction, and there is correspondingly less research on them.

Studying the various forms of creative sign language and their origins offers possibilities for translation or interpretation, especially when translating from sign languages to spoken languages. To help the target audiences appreciate that they are seeing a work of a particular genre, such as a poem, translators may opt to create a translation that follows recognised poetic norms in the target culture, even though the poetic elements are not present in the source language. Thus, for example, a signed poem's translation may be written in lines or may contain rhyme or alliteration. This can give the creative sign language additional status in the eyes of the target language audience.

We have seen that translating written haiku poems in languages like English and Portuguese into sign languages helped to create the signed haiku genre, but translation in the opposite direction is also possible, although not so common. Researcher and translator Marcus Weininger translated the Libras haiku poem *Peixe* by Renato Nunes into Portuguese haiku (Weininger & Sutton-Spence 2015). Although the linguistic elements are different in the two languages, translating a haiku poem in Libras into the equivalent genre in Portuguese was an important and historic step which recognised that the work really was haiku.

Kenny Lerner, an American poet who works as half of the duo Flying Words Project, recommends that translator-interpreters can use 'selective translation' so that the speech that accompanies highly visual ASL poems simply gives 'hints', enough for the hearing audience to follow the visual performance of the deaf poet (Spooner et al. 2018). Sometimes, just a word or a short, grammatically incomplete sentence is enough to help the non-signers identify the referent and from there, they can follow the visual images. This new development in literary translation is just one example of the growth and evolution of the entire field of creative sign language.

Our necessarily brief and selective review of genres in creative sign language has demonstrated the rich diversity of work that has been produced by deaf language artists worldwide. We have seen that genres may be based on several key principles, such as origin, form, function, and target audience. Genres may also be determined by their themes and topics. The final section of this Element now turns to the themes and topics in creative sign language, so we may explore the question 'What is Deaf Literature about?'

## 4 Themes and Content in Creative Sign Language

Themes in deaf literature and sign language literature can be seen in the content of stories and narratives, poems, jokes, and other humorous forms and theatre. We also need to consider the content of deaf non-fiction and deaf fiction, thinking about the emotions, intentions, and more abstract, less visible themes behind the content of the pieces. Stories or poems may be about all sorts of topics, but there are often other, larger, more abstract, themes and symbolism behind them.

Themes in written deaf literature and signed deaf literature have different profiles. Thinking about the four key characteristics of deaf literature that we outlined at the beginning of this Element, we see that there is a different emphasis on the four fundamental criteria of 'produced by deaf people, for deaf people, about deaf people, and in the language (sign language) of deaf people'. Deaf literature written in the language of the surrounding hearing society is principally marked as deaf literature because deaf people wrote it, and the topic relates directly to deafness. In signed deaf literature, the primary characteristics are that it is aimed at deaf people in the language of deaf people. Thus, we may expect that the themes of the two genres will be different, although we emphasise that no deaf literature exists without members of the deaf community.

Peixoto (2016, p. 79) has observed that one of the main sources for research on themes in deaf literature has been published books written by deaf people. Müller and Karnopp (2015) made similar observations. Written texts are especially important because they are the most easily accessible to hearing people who may read them, to learn about deaf culture. The books contributed to developing research in deaf studies. However, although such books are important for representing deaf people in the context of deaf literature, because they are written in the language of the hearing majority, they bring into focus the question of language and power. Our deaf literature that represents deaf culture is in sign language, a language of which we are proud, and we need to bring this to hearing people. This way, sign language literature can be included in the general concept of what is understood as 'literature', rather than as something separate, and other cultures can see and appreciate deaf pride in deaf literature in sign language. All the different genres of literature – stories, poems, jokes, and theatre – can be seen in deaf people's language, showing its richness, promoting all the positive aspects of deaf life through the literature of the deaf community. This is why language – sign language – is at the heart of deaf literature and it can resist the oppression of the majority spoken language (Portuguese in the case of Libras in Brazil), by showing the expressivity and creativity of deaf individuals using sign language.

Peixoto (2016, p. 183) emphasises that deaf people's writing for hearing readership tends to focus on deaf people's needs, asking for help and support from hearing people, and focusing on the 'hearing loss' aspects of deafness and other negative things associated with deafness. Many deaf people suffer from the insecurity of uncertainty in producing this type of literature, wondering if, as a deaf person, they are capable of writing something that will be respected by the hearing world. The written texts are often about the oppression of deaf people caused by the medical model of deficiency of deaf people, fighting to be seen as equal to hearing people and beset by uncertainties and emotional agitation. For some deaf people, the way to express this is to put it on paper, not necessarily as a personal account but as an individual's way of expressing a collective experience for hearing people to see.

For example, Shirley Vilhava's (2004) book *Waking from Silence*[93] covers the difficulties and anxieties she felt during the negative period of her life in her early years and the pride that followed in discovering her deaf identity and her practical experiences, showing the positive aspects of deaf awareness and leadership. A hearing readership can learn about the importance of sign language from reading such accounts written in their own language, and this can bring the deaf community and hearing society closer. Deaf literature can show the positive side of deaf living such as pride and celebration, valorisation of being a deaf person, resistance and leadership but also the oppression and prejudice that deaf people face, and the threats to their language and culture. Sometimes, these themes are overt and at others they are more hidden, for example through metaphors.

All these themes are also expressed in sign language literature by deaf people, which is why it is so important to encourage people to express these themes also through sign language.

## Thematic Organisation of Recorded Deaf Literature

The first theme we will consider is that of audism, or the unstated acceptance by many people (some deaf, as well as hearing) that to be able to hear is desirable and superior and that deafness is undesirable and inferior. This was the theme of *That's Life*,[94] a theatrical piece by CIACS, the Centre for Integration of Deaf Art and Culture[95] at INES in 1993. This work was performed in the early years of the Brazilian deaf literary scene in the 1980s and 1990s and caught the attention of the deaf community. At that time, the themes were more negative, although there were a few instances of more positive views of deaf people. *That's Life*

---

[93] In Portuguese, *Despertar do Silêncio.*     [94] In Portuguese, *A Vida como ela é.*
[95] *Centro de integração de arte e cultura surda.*

was a serious piece, based on the realities of deaf people's difficult everyday experiences at that time, with an underlying message that these were unacceptable, for example, that deaf people shouldn't have relationships with each other or marry. As Sutton-Spence et al. (2017) noted from interviews with Brazilian deaf Libras artists about their experiences, at that time, audism was sufficiently powerful that audiences who saw the performance were astonished, never having thought about their oppression in this way.

A deaf actor, Nelson Pimenta, published the first VHS tape (later transferred to DVD) entitled *Literature in LSB* with the company LSB Video, containing original poems, deaf-authored fables, and classic children's stories in Libras. This was the first publication of sign language literature in Brazil, in 1999. It showed that Libras literature existed, what poems in Libras were, and what fables and stories in Libras could be like. The collection was hugely important because until then there had been no formal recognition of creative, artistic Libras. Nelson Pimenta's publication caused a revolution in deaf people's understanding of Deaf Literature, as many people who had been unaware of it suddenly saw highly polished sign language poetry and storytelling. Some pieces were translations, for example of fables and children's classics, but the poems were original, directly from the deaf perspective. Their themes included pride in being Brazilian and in being deaf, deaf people's capacity to express themselves through sign language, and the comparison and contrast between signing and speaking, stemming from the creativity of a deaf person's view. Nelson Pimenta's theme of Being Deaf came from his time spent learning from the North American deaf community, and the poems in his DVD pay homage to the ASL artists there who supported the development of his work and thus, for the rest of Brazil.

Nelson Pimenta's translations of fables and children's classics (such as *Little Red Riding Hood* and *Pinocchio*) proved that deaf people are highly capable translators, using the facial expression and embodiment needed to produce strongly visual performances that attracted and enchanted child audiences. His telling of the fables and stories became the benchmark for future translations and retellings of children's literature.

The theme of deaf people's experiences is especially common in deaf theatre, especially in traditional, informal productions. Collectively constructed, only very loosely scripted shows were put on at deaf clubs. One example is *Bus Stop*, in which deaf people standing in a bus queue signed their stories of experience as deaf people to each other. Another example is *Crazy Comic Strips*[96] by Marlene Prado, Carlos Goes, and Silas Queiroz in Rio de Janeiro with

---

[96] In Portuguese, *Quadrinhos malucos*.

a theme of communication barriers for deaf people. Both these productions dealt with the real-life experiences of deaf people in the 1990s.

In an interview conducted for the research project 'Folklore and Deaf Literature in sign language: Deaf Brazilian artists tell their stories'[97] (Sutton-Spence et al. 2017), Silas Queiroz referred to *Bus Stop* and *Crazy Comic Strips* and provided photographs of the performances in the 1990s. These photos are also available as historical documents in the anthology of poetic Libras collected by Machado in 2017.

A key theme in written Deaf Literature, published as books in text form, following the set of criteria identified by Peixoto (2016), is the physical condition of deafness, although deaf identity and deaf people's abilities and capabilities is also important. When these books are written in the language of the surrounding hearing society, they bring deaf people's experiences to hearing people, although if the texts are written clearly and accessibly, and with illustrations, deaf people can enjoy reading them too. The books are important for encouraging empathy and understanding for deaf people's often trying and stressful experiences.

The edited collections *The Sound of Words*[98] (2003), *My feelings on leaves*[99] (Oliveira 2005), and *Poetic Butterflies*[100] (Rosa 2017) also focus on physical aspects of deafness, deaf identity, and the challenges to deaf people's well-being. Despite the span of time between 2003 and 2017, the issues covered in these texts are the same, as deaf people still have to face feelings of insecurity and uncertainty about their identity and self-worth, dealing with questions of choosing between cochlear implants, hearing aids, and oralism or sign language – topics that relate to the bigger theme of audism – that are part of the reality of deaf experience.

*The Hidden Lament of a Deaf Person*[101] (2004) written in Portuguese by Shirley Vilhalva but translated into Libras and performed by different deaf people, speaks openly to an imagined hearing person about the sufferings and injustices imposed upon deaf people by hearing people. These themes persist. The lament refers to tears, cries, complaints, and other topics that Peixoto (2016) sees as part of the category of the focus on the physical side of deafness and deaf identity and the worries and distress that this can cause.

Some written texts by deaf people are bilingual texts that are written in the community's spoken and signed languages, the latter through writing systems,

---

[97] In Portuguese, *Folclore e Literatura Surda em Língua de Sinais: os artistas surdos Brasileiros contam suas histórias.*

[98] In Portuguese, *O Som das Palavras* (no author or editor identified).

[99] In Portuguese, *Meus sentimentos em folhas.*     [100] In Portuguese, *Borboletas poéticas.*

[101] In Portuguese, *Lamento oculto de um surdo.*

especially SignWriting. This is especially the case in educational texts for deaf children in Brazil, and the two texts in Portuguese and Libras are usually complemented by illustrations. These bilingual texts have deaf characters, and themes of deafness and sign language are common. *Tibi and Joca* by Claudia Bisol (2011) is a children's book that celebrates deafness. Tibi is a deaf child, the only deaf person in his family, who meets a friendly alien from another planet who is also deaf and shows him how to overcome the challenges he faces, to become proud and happy to be deaf. We can see in this book (and others in the genre) the theme of deaf people overcoming difficulties of being a deaf person in a hearing world.

Adapted bilingual texts include *Deaf Cinderella* by Hessel Silveira, Karnopp, and Rosa (2005), *Deaf Rapunzel* by the same authors (2005), *The Deaf Duckling* by Karnopp and Rosa (2005), and *The Deaf Cicada and the Ants* by Oliveira and Boldo (n.d.).[102] These and other texts were presented and analysed as part of the highly influential course materials for the first course in Deaf Literature taught in Brazil by Lodenir Karnopp in 2008 that was part of the degree course in Brazilian Sign Language studies, that has since been studied by at least 2,000 undergraduates nationwide. The adaptations added the theme of deaf experiences, especially the use of sign language, turning the stories into deaf stories that can be owned by deaf people. Despite a lack of original deaf stories in picture books for young deaf pupils, these adaptations add an inclusive deaf perspective to the existing stories.

As deaf people have begun to film and make available increasing amounts of original deaf work in sign language, researchers have been able assemble larger collections to analyse them for their form and content, with emerging themes to be described.

A theme running through Deaf Literature is 'the collective'. This is frequently seen in canonical examples of literature in sign language (compared to the focus on individual anguish described in the written texts we have described). Stories, poems, jokes, and theatrical and dance pieces all contain this theme, especially when they occur at large events such as deaf festivals, for example the Festival of Deaf Folklore held in Florianópolis in 2014 and 2016. The pieces performed there were filmed and are preserved and made available through the UFSC video database repository, representing seminal deaf literary artists of humour, poetry, and storytelling (Sutton-Spence et al. 2016). Much of the work performed in Libras at these large collective events describes the collective experience of the deaf self, deaf feeling, and deaf behaviour that deaf audiences at these group

---

[102] In Portuguese, *Cinderela Surda, Rapunzel surda, o Patinho surdo* and *A cigarra surda e as formigas*.

events can appreciate and reflect upon. Recordings of another collective series of literary events, made by the Art of Signing[103] series at the Federal University of Rio Grande do Sul, show similar themes.

Christie and Wilkins (2007) considered the themes and symbolism seen in deaf art, especially ASL poetry produced in the 1990s and early twenty-first century. They found four themes that centred on language, education, personal identity, and social experiences of deaf people, identifying themes of deaf resistance to oppression and the liberation that follows. The linguistic issues frequently related to questions of language and power and the value of language, such as the struggles with English and oralism. For example, an ASL poem by Debbie Rennie describes the frustrations of her experience of using her residual hearing and trying to lipread in school. Educational issues referred to the historical oppression of sign languages as hearing society insisted on oralism and speech for deaf children. Patrick Graybill's poem describes his suffering with English, the physical restrictions imposed by his school to prevent him from signing and the freedom that comes from sign language. Personal identity describes the rich experience of using sign language and the value of sign language expressed as a deaf person's love for their language, as seen in a poem by Clayton Valli. Social themes arise because most deaf people's families do not know sign language, creating communication barriers, as seen in poems by Clayton Valli and Ella Mae Lentz.

In deaf humour and jokes, Hessel Silveira (2015) found that one of the principal recurring themes was communication problems between deaf and hearing people – problems that are usually solved by sign language. The jokes provoke people to think through the issues of language and communication for deaf people. When sign language is the solution to many of the problems set up in the jokes, we can see examples of the theme of 'Deaf Gain' (Bauman & Murray 2014) in which so-called hearing loss is transformed as the positive benefits of being deaf are offered to deaf people to learn from. We should note that these deaf jokes are traditional jokes that have been around in the community for many years.

It is important to remember that themes in any literature change over time as the social contexts of the work change. Crucially for Brazilian Deaf Literature, the changes that occurred after the Libras Law of 2002 officially recognising Libras and its enacting decree of 2005 that protected its use in education and public life permitted the nationwide Letras Libras Sign Language Studies courses. With the changing social situation of Brazilian deaf people, the themes of Deaf Literature and Libras literature changed.

---

[103] In Portuguese, *Arte de Sinalizar*, www.ufrgs.br/artedesinalizar/.

It seems that the themes identified by researchers in one country have parallels in other countries. For example, Sutton-Spence and Quadros (2005) compared original sign language poems by a Brazilian and a British deaf artist on their respective national flags as they both address the theme of national cultures as deaf people.

Peixoto (2016) collected examples of original deaf poetry in Libras, all from the twenty-first century, from across the whole of Brazil. Of the seventy works that she analysed for their themes, she found that twenty-six (37%) involved the Deaf World, thirteen were on religious themes, twelve on commemorative dates, seven on love, four on the nation, three on nature, and five on other themes. Within the theme of Deaf World, there were topics such as deaf culture, sign language, homage to figures within the deaf community, institutions such as the National Deaf School INES, university courses on sign language studies, deaf clubs, deaf education, and cochlear implants. All these Deaf World themes are examples of deaf experiences expressed through original deaf poetry.

Peixoto's (2016) analysis of Libras literature identified a theme of commemorative dates in the annual calendar. The poem *Christmas Tree*[104] by Fernanda Machado (on DVD, 2005) takes as its theme a celebratory moment in the calendar which makes up part of the rhythm of people's lives, such as Mothers' Day, Fathers' Day, and Children's Day. Christmas, though, is perhaps the most special calendar event and celebrating this in highly visual sign language, with creative use of classifiers and aesthetic signing had a strong impact on other deaf people. The poem was used widely in schools with children because it presents its story so visually, and it appealed to deaf and hearing people alike, especially because it was presented with other images – including a real Christmas tree. Similarly, Bruno Ramos' version of the Brazilian national anthem in Libras and Nelson Pimenta's Libras poem *Brazilian Flag* celebrate Independence Day and the Proclamation of the Republic, other important days in the national Brazilian calendar. All of them bring the delight of portraying this in sign language, presenting observations on it visually, and highlighting details through use of classifiers and other visually aesthetic signing.

Morgan and Kaneko (2018) analysed the thematic and related features of South African Sign Language (SASL) poetry. They found that the SASL poetry they reviewed was distributed across three key themes of deafhood, nationhood, and nature.[105] This contrasts with previous findings about the literature of American or European sign languages, which have mostly focused on deaf identity.

---

[104] In Portuguese, *Árvore de Natal.*
[105] See, for example *Avocado* by Modiegi Njeyiyana https://vimeo.com/196566449.

The Anthology of Literature in Libras described in Section 1 collected works that were divided into three categories of original deaf poetry, stories of deaf origin, and stories of non-deaf origin. Within those categories, guided by Bahan's (2006) description of ASL literature, we can see that there are themes of deaf perspectives, the relationship between the deaf and hearing worlds, communication and the oppression and celebration of sign language. However, works in sign language also focus on other important issues of identity in the broader sense.

The themes found in didactic literature aim to teach children what is 'proper' feeling and behaviour, as understood by adults within their society, through the actions and the consequences of these actions of characters that the children can relate to (Czechowski 2008; Froid 2016). Within the anthology mentioned in Section 1 is a subcollection of original deaf stories created for very young deaf children as part of the UFSC didactic literature project (2018–21). These are deliberately humorous short stories about the incongruous activities of different animals (and a banana) designed to teach young deaf children about the structure of their language but also what is good and moral behaviour. The characters are all understood to be deaf and behave in a range of different ways that are designed to amuse the children, but which adults can also use to discuss behaviour. ('Why was the ant embarrassed?' 'Was the gorilla right to take the motorbike?' 'Why do the deaf bees need to be careful near the traffic?' 'How did the dog feel when he scored that winning basketball point?'). They also address the deaf experiences such as the relationship between the deaf and hearing worlds and communication, but deliberately do not address themes of oppression.

Sutton-Spence (2019, 2021) has also highlighted the recent emergence of themes of feminism within Deaf Literature, including oppression and violence against women, and freedom and equality for women. Feminist themes in Libras poetry were highlighted in a 2022 issue of the interview series 'Dialogues on Libras Literature' (coordinated by the two authors and Marilyn Klamt, and available through the TV UFSC YouTube channel) through interviews with three deaf women poets, Cristiane Esteves de Andrade,[106] Priscila Leonnor,[107] and Renata Freitas.[108] Many of their poems address feminist themes without explicitly mentioning deafness, but as they are expressed from their perspective as deaf poets in sign language and are aimed primarily at an audience of deaf women, they bring these themes to the deaf community. Priscila Leonnor strongly identifies as a black deaf woman and, similarly, many of her poems also refer to

---

[106] https://youtu.be/1xCtrzpIt64.    [107] https://youtu.be/ZJLZsx7l8zw.
[108] https://youtu.be/PWgTEfnae1A.

the resistance and strength of black Brazilian women in general (including, it is understood, deaf women), rather than specifically deaf black Brazilian women.

Campos (2017) has also considered themes of regional identity in Brazil, from the perspective of the deaf community. The genre of Cordel literature, especially recognised by its rhythmic and rhyme forms, is strongly associated with the north-east of Brazil but due to its complex and primarily oral form is largely inaccessible to deaf people (Sutton-Spence & Campos 2019). As a deaf poet from the region, Campos has encouraged deaf people to create their own 'cordel' in Libras, in which the theme is the experience of north-easterners, but from a deaf perspective, and the theme defines the genre, rather than the form.

In our exploration of creative sign language in this Element, we have cited forty-six examples of poems, stories, and jokes in different sign languages but primarily in Libras, and mostly created since 2010. Of these, thirteen have themes clearly related to deafness or sign language. Another three do not mention deafness, but audiences are expected to know that the story presented refers to deaf people (*Bird of a Different Feather, Doll* and Paul Scott's *Tree*). A further three do not have central deaf or sign language-related themes but have deaf characters that use sign language (*Party, Ball Story* and *The Deaf Cow in High Heels*). All these may be categorised as relating to the theme of Deaf World, as described in Peixoto. This is approximately 40 per cent of our selection (admittedly chosen from a far larger corpus as examples that contain something interesting in their form or as representatives of their genre). It means that nearly 60 per cent of the examples, although performed in aesthetically rich sign language, do not have especially deaf themes. These figures are not much different from Peixoto's and show the broad range of topics and themes addressed by deaf artists working with their sign languages more than two decades into the twenty-first century.

## Conclusion

Creative sign language is extraordinarily diverse in its form and its themes. It shows the potential of deaf people and sign languages to create playful, emotional, witty, elegant, and frequently breath-taking visual linguistic artforms. Creative sign language is more than texts and cultural artefacts. It is an ever-changing process, made by action, performance, and engagement between the artists and their audiences.

We have seen in this necessarily selective review how sign language literatures share many characteristics with the written literatures produced by hearing societies, but by taking a bottom-up as well as top-down approach, we have seen how the specific characteristics of the visual art form in the hands of deaf people (who are a visual people, or 'a people of the eye'[109]) brings a new dimension to any understanding of what literature is and what literature could be.

By studying the history and social context of creative signing we can see how crucial the deaf community is for its development. Social, educational, legal, and technological changes all impact powerfully on this rapidly changing and developing form of language art but the hard work, determination, and talent of individual members of the deaf community, aided by hearing allies, have contributed to the collective, worldwide phenomenon that is currently understood as Deaf Literature or creative sign language.

By paying close attention to deaf artists' manipulation of language to produce this artform, we expand our understanding of what 'sign language' means. We can see how current theories and understanding of language and literature can be informed by, and need to account for, what deaf artists do with sign language and its performance.

There is no doubt that members of hearing society with any interest in literature and language art need to know about and understand the significance of the work of deaf language artists, whether storytellers, poets, humourists, VV artists, or unclassifiable performers. As the ASL performer Peter Cook observed: 'modern poets are amazed when they see ASL poetry. Because they strive to take images and put them into language – let the words become pictures. That's what we do in ASL poetry' (Peter Cook in Nathan Lerner & Feigel 2009, 00:08:58).

We began this Element with a quotation from *Language for the Eye* by the pioneering deaf sign language poet Dorothy Miles: 'The word becomes the picture in this language for the eye.' In sign language literature, through the 'visible bodily actions' of deaf artists, the words become pictures and the pictures come to life. We end here, then, with the final line of that poem: 'The word becomes the action in this language of the heart.'[110] The actions of sign language artists and their audiences keep that heart beating. We hope this Element can help to make the heartbeat a little stronger.

---

[109] As the deaf American George Veditz famously signed in ASL in 1912 (Lane et al. 2010).
[110] Language for the eye, Dorothy Miles, in *Gestures*, 1976.

# References

Aarons, D. & Morgan, R. (2003). Classifier predicates and the creation of multiple perspectives in South African Sign Language. *Sign Language Studies*, **3**, 125–56.

Andrews, J. F. & S. Baker, S. (2019). ASL nursery rhymes: Exploring a support for signing deaf children: Early language and emergent literacy skills. *Sign Language Studies*, 20, 5–40.

Asmal, A. & Kaneko, K. (2020). Visual vernacular in South African Sign Language. *Sign Language Studies*, **20**(3), 491–571.

Bahan, B. (1994). Comment on Turner. *Sign Language Studies*, **83**, 241–9.

Bahan, B. (2006). Face-to-face tradition in the American Deaf community. In H.-D. Bauman, J. Nelson & H. Rose, eds., *Signing the Body Poetic*. California: University of California Press, pp. 21–50.

Baldwin, S. (1993). *Pictures in the Air: The Story of the National Theater of the Deaf*. Washington, DC: Gallaudet University Press.

Barreto, M. & Barreto, R. (2015). *Escrita de Sinais sem mistérios* 2nd ed. Salvador: Libras Escrita.

Barros, R. O. (2020). *Tradução de poesia escrita em libras para a língua portuguesa*. Master's dissertation. Programa de Pós-Graduação em Estudos da Tradução. Florianópolis: Universidade Federal de Santa Catarina.

Bartolomei, N. P. R. & Pereira, V. C. (2021). Produções performáticas em libras: o uso do corpo e da máquina em produções literárias em língua brasileira de sinais. In A. Moraes da Costa, G. Marques & P. E. B. Moraes, eds., *Reconfigurações da literatura contemporânea: abordagens críticas*. Porto Velho: Coleção Pós Graduação da UNIR EDUFRO, pp. 52–64.

Battison, R. (1978). *Lexical Borrowing in American Sign Language*. Silver Spring, MD: Linstok Press.

Bauman, H.-D. (2003). Redesigning literature: The cinematic poetics of American Sign Language poetry. *Sign Language Studies*, **4**, 34–47.

Bauman, H.-D. (2006). Getting out of line: Toward a visual and cinematic poetics of ASL. In H.-D. Bauman, J. Nelson & H. Rose, eds., *Signing the Body Poetic*. California: University of California Press, pp. 95–117.

Bauman, D. & Murray, J. eds. (2014). *The New Normal: Deaf Gain and the Future of Human Diversity*. Minneapolis, MN: University of Minnesota Press.

Bergson, H. (1911). *Laughter: An Essay on the Meaning of the Comic*. English translation, 2003. London: MacMillan.

BISOL, C. (2001). *Tibi e Joca: uma história de dois mundos.* Porto Alegre: Mercado Aberto.

Blondel, M. & Miller, C. (2001). Movement and rhythm in nursery rhymes in LSF. *Sign Language Studies*, **2**(1), 24–61.

Boldo, J. & Sutton-Spence, R. (2020). Libras Humor: Playing with the Internal Structure of Signs. *Sign Language Studies*, **20**(3), 411–33.

Bourgeois, N. (2020). La Signographie. Poésies Sourdes. Les enjeux des traductions en LSF. *Revue GPS* n°11. Editions Plaine page.

Campos, K. (2017). *Literatura de cordel em Libras: os desafios de tradução da literatura nordestina pelo tradutor surdo.* Master's dissertation. Programa de Pós-Graduação em Estudos da Tradução da. Florianópolis: Universidade Federal de Santa Catarina.

Carmel, S. J. (1996). Deaf folklore. In J. H. Brunvand, ed., *American Folklore: An Encyclopedia.* New York: Garland, pp. 197–200.

Carvalho, D. R. (2018). *Metáfora em libras: Um estudo de léxico.* Master's dissertation. Programa de Pós-graduação em Linguística. Florianópolis: Universidade Federal de Santa Catarina.

Castro, N. P. (1999). *Literatura em LSB, LSB vídeo (DVD).* Rio de Janeiro: Editora Abril e Dawn Sign Press.

Catteau, F. (2020). *Traduire la poésie en langue des sign: L'empreinte prosodique lors du changement de modalité.* Doctoral dissertation. Paris: University of Paris 8. www.afcp-parole.org/wp-content/uploads/2021/01/These_CATTEAU_2020.pdf.

Christie, K. & Wilkins, C. (2007). Themes and symbols in ASL poetry: Resistance, affirmation and liberation. *Deaf Worlds*, **22**(3), 1–49.

Compagnon, A. (1999). *O demônio da teoria: literatura e senso comum.* Belo Horizonte: Ed. UFMG.

Crasborn, O. (1995). *Articulatory Symmetry in Two-handed Signs.* Master's dissertation. Department of General Linguistics. Nijmegen: University of Nijmegen.

Cuxac, C. (2000). *La Langue des Signes Françaises; les voies de l'iconicite.* Paris: Ophrys.

Cuxac, C. & Sallandre, M.-A. (2007). Iconicity and arbitrariness in French Sign Language: Highly iconic structures, degenerated iconicity and grammatic iconicity. In E. Pizzuto, P. Pietrandrea & S. Raffaele, eds., *Verbal and Signed Languages: Comparing Structure, Constructs and Methodologies.* Berlin: Mouton de Gruyter, pp. 13–33.

Czechowski, J. (2008). Functions of didactic children's and youth literature. *Kultura i Edukacja*, **5**(69), 74–90.

Dudis, P. (2004). Body partitioning and real-space blends. *Cognitive Linguistics*, **15**(2), 223–38.

Dudis, P. (2007). *Types of Depiction in ASL*. Washington, DC: Gallaudet University Press.

Dundes, A. (1965). What is Folklore? In A. Dundes, ed., *The Study of Folklore*. Englewood Cliffs, NJ: Prentice Hall, pp. 1–6.

Ferrara, L., & Johnston, T. (2014). Elaborating who's what: A study of constructed action and clause structure in Auslan (Australian Sign Language). *Australian Journal of Linguistics*, 34(2), 193–215.

Frishberg, N. (1988). Signers of tales: The case of literary status of an unwritten language. *Sign Language Studies*, 17(59), 149–70.

Froid, D. (2016). *Didactic Children's Literature and the Emergence of Animal Rights*. Master's dissertation. Bristol: University of Nebraska.

Guerini, A., Torres, M. H., & Costa, W. eds. (2011). *Literatura & tradução: textos selecionados de José Lambert*. Rio de Janeiro: 7Letras.

Hessel C. S. (2015). *Literatura Surda: análise da circulação de piadas clássicas em Língua de Sinais*. Doctoral dissertation. Porto Alegre: Universidade Federal do Rio Grande do Sul.

Hessel, C. S. & Karnopp, L. (2016). Humor na cultura surda: análise de piadas. *Textura*, 18(37), 169–89.

Hessel, C. S., Karnopp, L., & Rosa, F. S. (2005). *Rapunzel surda*. Canoas: Ed. ULBRA.

Hutcheon, L. (2012). *A Theory of Adaptation*. London: Routledge.

Johnston, T. & Schembri, A. (2007). *Australian Sign Language (Auslan): An Introduction to Sign Language Linguistics*. Cambridge: Cambridge University Press.

Júnior, F. V. de Souza & Pereira, V. C. (2020). Slam Surdo: análise das dimensões política e poética na performance 'O mudinho', de Edinho Santos. *Texto Poético*, 16(31), 6–25.

Kaneko, M. (2008). *The Poetics of Sign Language Haiku*. Doctoral dissertation. Bristol: University of Bristol.

Kaneko, M. & Mesch, J. (2013). Eye gaze in creative sign language. *Sign Language Studies*, 13 (3), 372–400.

Karnopp, L. (2008). *Literatura Surda*. Licenciatura em Letras-Libras na Modalidade a Distância. Florianópolis: UFSC.

Karnopp, L. & Rosa, F. S. (2005). *O Patinho Surdo*. Canoas: Ed. ULBRA.

Karnopp, L. B., Klein, M., & Lunardi-Lazzarin, M. L. (2011). Produção, circulação e consumo da cultura surda brasileira. In L. B. Karnopp, M. Klein & M. Lunardi-Lazzarin, eds., *Cultura Surda Na Contemporaneidade: Negociações, Intercorrências E Provocações*. Canoas: Ed. ULBRA, pp. 15–28.

Kendon, A. (2017). Languages as semiotically heterogenous systems. *Behavioral and Brain Sciences*, 40, 30–1.

Klima, E. & Bellugi, U. (1979). *The Signs of Language*. Cambridge, MA: Harvard University Press.

Krentz, C. (2006). The camera as printing press: How film has influenced ASL literature. In H.-D. Bauman, J. Nelson & H. Rose, eds., *Signing the Body Poetic*. California: University of California Press, pp. 51–70.

Kusters, A. & Sahasrabudhe, S. (2018). Language Ideologies on the Difference Between Gesture and Sign. *Language and Communication*, **60**, 44–63.

Kusters, A., Spotti M., Swanwick, R., & Tapio, E. (2017). Beyond languages, beyond modalities: Transforming the Study of semiotic repertoires. *International Journal of Multilingualism*, 14(3), 1–14.

Ladd, P. (2002). *Understanding Deaf Culture: In Search of Deafhood*. Clevedon: Multilingual Matters.

Lakoff, G. & Johnson, M. (1980). *Metaphors We Live By*. Chicago, IL: University of Chicago Press.

Lane, H., Hoffmeister, R., & Bahan, B. (1996). *A Journey into the DEAF WORLD*. San Diego, CA: Dawn Sign Press.

Lane, H., Pillard, R. C., & Hedberg, U. (2010). *The People of the Eye: Deaf Ethnicity and Ancestry*. Oxford: Oxford University Press.

Leech, G. (1969). *A Linguistic Guide to English Poetry*. London: Longman.

Leitch, V. (2004). Ideology of Headnotes. In J. Di Leo, ed., *On Anthologies: Politics and Pedagogy*. Lincoln, NE: University of Nebraska Press, pp. 373–83.

Luckner, J., & Yarger, C. (1997). What's so funny?: A comparison of students who are deaf or hard of hearing and hearing students' appreciation of cartoons. *American Annals of the Deaf*, 142(5), 373–8.

Machado, F. (2005). *Poesia Árvore de Natal*. Rio de Janeiro: LSB vídeo.

Machado, F. (2013). *Simetria na Poética Visual na Língua de Sinais Brasileira*. Master's dissertation. Programa de Pós-Graduação em Estudos da Tradução. Florianópolis: Universidade Federal de Santa Catarina.

Machado, F. (2017). *Antologia da poética de Língua de Sinais Brasileira*. Doctoral dissertation. Programa de Pós-Graduação em Estudos da Tradução. Florianópolis: Universidade Federal de Santa Catarina.

Machado, F. (2019). Representing Libras poetry on video. *Altre Modernità*, **22**, 25–7. https://riviste.unimi.it/index.php/AMonline/article/view/12409/11686.

Marquezi, L. (2018). *Literatura surda: o processo de tradução e transcrição em SignWriting*. Master's dissertation. Programa de Pós-Graduação em Estudos da Tradução. Florianópolis: Universidade Federal de Santa Catarina.

Metzger, M. (1995). Constructed dialogue and constructed action in American Sign Language. In C. Lucas, ed., *Sociolinguistics in Deaf Communities*. Washington, DC: Gallaudet University Press, pp. 255–71.

Miles, D. (1976). *Gestures: Poetry in Sign Language*. Northridge, CA: Joyce Motion Picture.

Miles, D. (1998). *Bright Memory*. Doncaster: British Deaf History Society.

Monteiro, C. J. (2023). *Um estudo da visual vernacular (VV): cultura e literatura surda em diálogo com a estética da recepção*. Master's dissertation. Programa de pós-graduação em linguagem e ensino. Campina Grande: Universidade Federal de Campina Grande.

Morgado, M. (2011). Literatura em língua gestual. In L. Karnopp, M. Klein & M. Lunardi-Lazzarin, eds., *Cultura Surda na contemporaneidade*. Canoas: Editora ULBRA, pp. 151–72.

Morgan, R. & Kaneko, M. (2018). Deafhood, nationhood and nature: Thematic analysis of South African Sign Language poetry. *South African Journal of African Languages*, **38**(3), 363–74.

Mourão, C. H. N. (2016). *Literatura surda: experiência das mãos literárias*. Doctoral dissertation. Programa de Pós-Graduação em Educação. Porto Alegre: Universidade Federal do Rio Grande do Sul.

Müller, J. I. & Karnopp, L. (2015). Cultural translation in education: Experiences of difference in deaf writing. *Educação e Pesquisa*, **41**(4), 1041–54.

Napoli, D. J. & Wu, J. (2003). Morpheme structure constraints on two-handed signs in American Sign Language: Notions of symmetry. *Journal of Sign Language and Linguistics*, **6**, 123–205.

Nathan Lerner, M. & Feigel, D. (2009). *The Heart of the Hydrogen Jukebox*. New York: Rochester Institute of Technology.

O Som das Palavras (no author or editor identified) (2003). *Antologia Literária*. Rio de Janeiro: Litteris Ed.

Oliveira, C. & Boldo, J. (undated). *A cigarra surda e as formigas*. Rio Grande do Sul: Corag.

Oliveira, R. (2005). *Meus sentimentos em folhas*. Rio de Janeiro: Editora Litteris.

Opie, I. & Opie, P. (1959). *The Lore and Language of Schoolchildren*. Oxford: Oxford University Press.

Pedroni, V. H. (2021). *Dueto de poesia em libras: os desafios de tradução da literatura pelo tradutor dueto*. Master's dissertation. Programa de Pós-Graduação em Estudos da Tradução. Florianópolis: Universidade Federal de Santa Catarina.

Peixoto, J. (2016). *O registro da beleza nas mãos: a tradição de produções poéticas em Língua de Sinais no Brasil*. Doctoral dissertation. Programa de Pós-Graduação em Letras da. João Pessoa: Universidade Federal da Paraíba.

Peters, C. (2000). *Deaf American Literature: From Carnival to the Canon*. Washington, DC: Gallaudet University Press.

Petry, D. B. & Fischer, G. B. (2014). Entre Méliès E Hollywood: Pistas Para Pensar Os Efeitos Visuais No Cinema a Partir Da Arqueologia Das mídias. *Animus: Revista Interamericana De Comunicação Midiática*, 13(25), 1–16.

Pichler, D. C., Stumpf, M. R., Quadros, R., Kuntze, M., & Lillo-Martin, D. (2019). *Aquisição Língua de Sinais*. Petrópolis: Editora Arara Azul. https://libras.ufsc.br/arquivos/vbooks/aquisição.

Quinto-Pozos, D. (2007). Can constructed action be considered obligatory? *Lingua*, **117**, 1285–314.

Reis, P. (1998). *Poesia Concreta: Uma Prática Intersemiótica*. Porto: Edições UFP.

Ribeiro, A. & Sutton-Spence, R. (2021). Ball, stone, ball: Interlingual, intramodal and intersemiotic translation between and from a work of creative sign language. *Cadernos de Tradução*, **41**, 250–72. In Libras at www.youtube.com/watch? v=DGLPzi7I7SE.

Rocha, S. (2008). *O INES e a educação de surdos no Brasil: aspectos da trajetória do Instituto Nacional de Educação de Surdos em seu percurso de 150 anos*. Rio de Janeiro: INES.

Rosa, E. (2017). *Borboletas Poéticas*. Porto Alegre: Vivilendo.

Rose, H. (1992). *A Critical Methodology for Analyzing American Sign Language Literature*. Doctoral dissertation. Tempe, AZ: Arizona State University.

Rose, H. (2006). The poet in the poem in the performance: The relation of body, self, and text in ASL literature. In H.-D. Bauman, J. Nelson & H. Rose, eds., *Signing the Body Poetic*. California: University of California Press, pp. 130–46.

Rutherford, S. (1989). Funny in Deaf: Not in hearing. In S. Wilcox, ed., *American Deaf Culture: An Anthology*. Silver Spring, MD: Linstok Press, pp. 65–82.

Rutherford, S. (1993). *A study of American Deaf folklore*. Burtonsville, MD: Linstok Press.

Ryan, S. (1993). Let's Tell an ASL Story. *Gallaudet University College for Continuing Education. Conference Proceedings*. Washington, D.C.: Gallaudet University Press, pp. 145–9.

Santos, R. de L., Grigolom, G., & Medeiros, J. (2020). Slam resistência surda – Curitiba: movimento e poesia. *INES Revista Espaço*, **54**, 31–53.

Schallenberger, A. (2010). *Ciberhumor nas comunidades surdas*. Master's Dissertation. UFRGS/FACED/PPGEDU. Porto Alegre: Universidade Federal de Rio Grande do Sul.

Schembri, A. (2003). Rethinking 'classifiers' in signed languages. In K. Emmorey, ed., *Perspectives on Classifier Constructions in Sign Languages*. Mahwah, NJ: Lawrence Erlbaum Associates, pp. 3–34.

Schlemper, M. D. (2021). Tradução comentada, de produção audiovisual em libras para o português escrito, do conto 'A Formiga Indígena Surda', de marina teles. *Revista GEMInIS*, **12**(3), 124–46.

Smith, A. K. & Jacobowitz, E. L. (2006). *Have You Ever Seen … ? An American Sign Language Handshape DVD/Book*. Cave Spring, GA: ASL Rose.

Smith, S. & Cormier, K. (2014). In or out? Spatial scale and enactment in narratives of native and non-native signing deaf children acquiring British Sign Language. *Sign Language Studies*, **14**, 275–301.

Spooner, R. A. (2016). *Languages, Literacies, and Translations: Examining Deaf Students' Language Ideologies Through English-to-ASL Translations of Literature* Ph.D. dissertation. Ann Arbor, MI: University of Michigan.

Spooner, R. A., Sutton-Spence, R., Nathan Lerner, M., & Lerner, K. (2018). Invisible no more: Recasting the role of the ASL-English literary translator. *Translation and Interpreting Studies*, **13**(1), 110–29.

Stewart, L. (1990). Sign Language: Some thoughts of a deaf American. In M. Garretson, ed., *Eyes, Hands and Voices: Communication issues among deaf people. A Deaf American Monograph*. Silver Spring: National Association of the Deaf, pp. 118.

Stone, C. (2009). *Toward a Deaf Translation Norm*. Washington, DC: Gallaudet University Press.

Strobel, K. (2013). *As imagens do outro sobre a cultura surda*. Florianópolis: Ed. Da UFSC.

Supalla, T. (1994). *Charles Krauel: A Profile of a Deaf Filmmaker*. Video tape. San Diego, CA: DawnPictures.

Sutton-Spence, R. (2019). Literatura surda feita por mulheres. In A. Batista, M. Dalvi, P. Dutra & W. Salgueiro, eds., *Literatura e artes, teoria e crítica feitas por mulheres*. Campos dos Goytacazes: Instituto Brasil Multicultural de Educação e Pesquisa – IBRAMEP, pp. 142–66.

Sutton-Spence, R. (2020). Literatura de Língua de Sinais, Educação Surda e suas interfaces com as políticas linguísticas. (Sign language literature, Deaf education and their interface with language policies). *Educação Unisinos*, **24**, 1–16.

Sutton-Spence, R. (2021). *Literatura em Libras*. Petrópolis: Arara Azul. (Full Libras translation at www.literaturaemlibras.com).

Sutton-Spence, R. & Campos, K. (2019). Translating cordel literature into libras: Some challenges for Deaf translators. *Sign Language Studies*, **19**(4), 491–518.

Sutton-Spence, R. & Kaneko, M. (2007). Symmetry in Sign Language poetry. *Sign Language Studies*, **7**(3), 284–318.

Sutton-Spence R. & Kaneko, M. (2016). *Introducing Sign Language Literature: Creativity and Folklore.* Basingstoke: Palgrave Press.

Sutton-Spence, R. & Machado, F. (2019). Considerations for creating anthologies of Sign Language poetry. *Sign Language Studies,* **19**(2), 267–94.

Sutton-Spence, R. & Napoli, D. J. (2012). Deaf jokes and sign language humour. *International Journal of Humor Research,* **25**(3), 311–38.

Sutton-Spence, R. & Quadros, R. (2005). Sign Language poetry and deaf identity. *Journal of Sign Language and Linguistics,* **8**, 177–212.

Sutton-Spence, R. & Woll, B. (1999). *The Linguistics of British Sign Language; An Introduction.* Cambridge: Cambridge University Press.

Sutton-Spence, R., Felício, M., Machado, F., et al. (2016). Os craques da Libras: a importância de um festival de folclore sinalizado. *Revista Sinalizar,* **1**(1), 78–92.

Sutton-Spence, R., Machado, F., Campos, K., et al. (2017). Artistas surdos contam suas histórias: quais foram suas influências? *Revista Brasileira de Vídeo Registros em Libras.* Video article, http://revistabrasileiravrlibras .paginas.ufsc.br/publicacoes/edicao-no-0032017/ (Edição Atual > Edição nº 003/2017).

Taylor, A. (1948). Folklore and the student of literature. In A. Dundes, ed., *The Study of Folklore.* Englewood Cliffs, NJ: Prentice Hall, pp. 34–42.

Valli, C. (1990). *Poetry in Motion.* Burtonsville, MD: Sign Media.

Van Brandwijk, M. (2018). *Visual Vernacular: A Inter and Intra Sign Language Poetry Genre Comparison.* Bachelor's dissertation. Leiden: University of Leiden.

Vilhalva, S. (2004). *Despertar do Silêncio.* Petrópolis/RJ: Arara Azul.

Weininger, M & Sutton-Spence, R. (2015). "Translating Sign Language Poetry". *5th IATIS Conference. Innovation paths in translation and intercultural studies.* Belo Horizonte: Federal University of Minas Gerais.

Weyl, H. (1952). *Symmetry.* Princeton, NJ: Princeton University Press.

Wilcox, S. & Lackner, A. (2021). Language is an 'activity of the whole body': A memorial to Franz Dotter. *Grazer Linguistische Studien,* **93**, 225–59.

# Acknowledgements

We would like to thank the series editors David Quinto-Pozos and Erin Wilkinson for their support during the production of this Element. Their involvement in the process and editorial comments on earlier drafts were invaluable. We are also grateful to the anonymous reviewers for their suggestions and advice and help in providing more international examples for this work. Our thanks, too, to the sign language artists who gave their kind permission for us to reproduce pictures of their work. Without them, the magic of this beautiful creative art form would not be so obvious. Obrigada, Thank you, Dankeschön and Hartelijk dank:

André Conceição, Angela Okumura, Anna Luiza Maciel, Cristiane Esteves de Andrade, Guiliano Robert, Gustavo Gusmão, João Raphael Bertoncelli, Juliana Tasca Lohn, Kácio Lima, Marcos Marquioto, Marina Teles, Martin Haswell, Mauricio Barreto, Nelson Pimenta Castro, Paul Scott, Ricardo Boaretto, Sara Amorim, Stefan Goldschmidt, Vanessa Lima.

# Sign Languages

## Erin Wilkinson

*University of New Mexico*

Erin Wilkinson is Associate Professor in the Department of Linguistics at the University of New Mexico. She has broad research interests in bilingualism and multilingualism, language documentation and description, language change and variation, signed language typology, and language planning and policy in highly diverse signing communities. Her current studies in collaboration with other researchers examine cognitive and linguistic processing in signing bilingual populations. She also explores what linguistic structures are re-structured over time in signed languages and what are possible factors that contribute to language change and variation in signed languages in the lens of usage-based theory.

## David Quinto-Pozos

*University of Texas at Austin*

David Quinto-Pozos is an Associate Professor in the Department of Linguistics at the University of Texas at Austin. His research interests include signed language contact and change, the interaction of language and gesture, L1 and L2 signed language acquisition, spoken-signed language interpretation, and vocabulary knowledge and literacy. He has served as an editor/co-editor of four volumes on signed language research, including *Modality and Structure in Signed and Spoken Languages* (Meier, Cormier, & Quinto-Pozos, eds. 2002; Cambridge University Press), *Sign Languages in Contact* (Quinto-Pozos, ed. 2007; Gallaudet University Press), *Multilingual Aspects of Signed Language Communication and Disorder* (Quinto-Pozos, 2014; Multilingual Matters), and *Toward Effective Practice: Interpreting in Spanish-influenced Settings* (Annarino, Aponte-Samalot, & Quinto-Pozos, 2014; National Consortium of Interpreter Education Centers).

## About the Series

This Elements series covers a broad range of topics on signed language structure and use, describing dozens of different signed languages, along with accounts of signing (deaf and non-deaf) communities. The series is accessible (via print, electronic media, and video-based summaries) to a large deaf/signing-friendly audience.

Cambridge Elements ⁼

# Sign Languages

---

### Elements in the Series

*A Family-Centered Signed Language Curriculum to Support Deaf Children's Language Acquisition*
Razi M. Zarchy and Leah C. Geer

*Creative Sign Language*
Rachel Sutton-Spence and Fernanda de Araújo Machado

Printed in the United States
by Baker & Taylor Publisher Services